MW01042054

COPENHAGEN

MANCHESTER
UNIVERSITY PRESS

The Buildings of Europe

Series advise-r: Christopher Woodward

Already published

Barcelona, Christopher Woodward
Berlin, Derek Fraser
Rome, Christopher Woodward

Forthcoming titles

Hanseatic Cities, Christoph Grafe
Prague, Jane Pavitt

The Buildings of Europe

COPENHAGEN

Christopher Woodward

Manchester University Press
Manchester and New York
Distributed exclusively in the USA by St. Martin's Press

Copyright © Christopher Woodward 1998

The right of Christopher Woodward to be identified as the author of this work has been asserted by him in accordance with the Copyright, Designs and Patents Act 1988.

Published by
Manchester University Press
Oxford Road, Manchester M13 9NR, UK
and
Room 400, 175 Fifth Avenue,
New York, NY 10010, USA

Distributed exclusively in the USA by
St. Martin's Press, Inc., 175 Fifth Avenue,
New York, NY 10010, USA

Distributed exclusively in Canada by
UBC Press, University of British Columbia, 6344
Memorial Road, Vancouver, BC, Canada V6T 1Z2

British Library Cataloguing-in-Publication data
A catalogue record for this book is available from the British Library

Library of Congress-Cataloging-in-Publication data
applied for

ISBN 0 7190 5192 4 hardback
ISBN 0 7190 5193 2 paperback

First published 1998

02 01 00 99 98   10 9 8 7 6 5 4 3 2 1

Typography by Nick Loat

Layout by the author

Printed in Great Britain by
Redwood Books, Trowbridge

How to use this guide

There are 185 *entries*—buildings, squares, engineering structures—arranged chronologically. Each entry has a *reference number*. This is followed by an uppercase letter which is the key to one of the two maps at the end of the book. Map A covers the 2.5 kilometres square of central Copenhagen, an area in which all the entries may be visited on foot. Map B shows a large part of outer Copenhagen, an area of 30 kilometres square. It is intended only to show the approximate position of the entries within its area and will need to be supplemented with a good street map. A lowercase letter follows the map letter: this indicates the smaller square on the map in which the entry is to be found. Where appropriate, the nearest underground ⊗ or regional ⊛ station is given. Underground stations in square brackets indicate a station under construction that may open in 1998 or 1999.

Some entries are followed by the symbol ☞. This means 'nearby' and the text following gives the reference number of entries which are nearby, and may mention other buildings which, while of some interest, do not warrant a fuller description. The symbol is also used on the maps to point to nearby entries on neighbouring maps.

Useful information on current events such as exhibitions and travel information can be had from the Tourist Information office on the corner of Bernstorffsgade and Vesterbrogade, opposite the Hovedbanegården, the main railway station.

The inclusion of a building in this guide does not mean that its grounds or interior are accessible. Please respect the privacy of those living or working in the buildings mentioned.

Contents

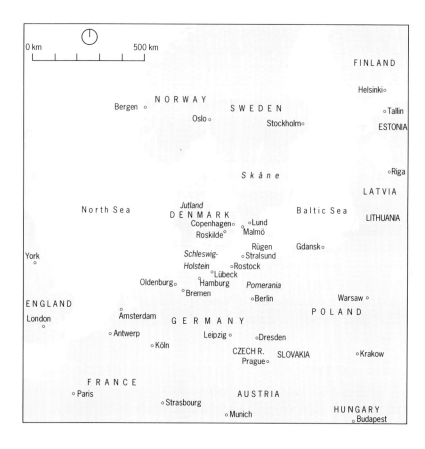

Introduction

Situated on the flat, sandy eastern edge of Sjælland, one of the larger of the many islands which are now included in the territory of the state of Denmark, Copenhagen has always commanded the main shipping route between the ports of the Baltic Sea and the oceans of the world: the narrow Øresund or 'Sound'. This strategic position and the availability of a small natural harbour sheltered by the island of Amager account for the existence in the eleventh century of a small fishing village on the site, then and still an island, Slotsholmen, now occupied by the present 'castle' Christiansborg **81**. At this time, the most important nearby centres of power in the region were the archbishoprics of Roskilde to the west of Copenhagen, and Lund to the east on the Swedish peninsula. The written history of Copenhagen starts in the twelfth century with the reign of King Valdemar 'the Great' (1157–82) who was first responsible for consolidating what was to become the state of Denmark. He fought the Saxons on the northern coast of Germany and the piratical Wends who occupied the island of Rügen, and came to control much of the Baltic coast together with the southern part of Sweden, Skåne or 'Scania'. Danish trade, mainly in salted herrings and formerly chiefly with England, became centred on the Baltic.

Foundations 1167
Valdemar gave the small village of Købmændenes Havn ('Merchants' Harbour'), later Copenhagen, to his foster-brother, Bishop Absalon of Roskilde, who in about 1167 built the circular defensive castle whose foundations **1** lie under Christiansborg, the former royal palace in the centre of the present city. Valdemar's successor, Knud IV, extended Danish territory to include much of northern Germany including Mecklenburg and Pomerania, and by the beginning of the thirteenth century later kings had pushed its boundaries further to incorporate much of northern Poland as far as its border with Estonia. In 1223, however, the Duke of Schwerin put a stop to this expansion

Introduction

and, in the first of the many reversals which Denmark has subsequently suffered, took away all the Baltic possessions. For the remainder of the thirteenth century the Kingdom of Denmark consisted of the Jutland peninsula and the islands to its east, settled by farmers and fishermen and administered from Copenhagen. During much of the fourteenth century, wars between the states and free cities surrounding the Baltic for control of the shipping and trade of the sea included the episode during which Copenhagen was invaded by the forces of Lübeck whose masons razed the castle. In 1370 these wars were concluded with the 'Peace of Stralsund'. In 1375, the crowns of Denmark and Norway were united, and in 1389 these two were consolidated with that of Sweden under Queen Margrethe I. By 1429, Denmark's military and naval position was secure enough to first levy the 'Sound Dues', a toll on all shipping passing through the Øresund.

In 1448, the Danish crown was offered to Christian I, of Oldenburg near the Hanseatic city of Bremen. This appointment reunited the territories of Denmark and Scania, their population of about a million, and established what became the Oldenburg dynasty which continued to provide Danish monarchs until 1863. His successors were, however, unable to prevent the secession of Sweden and in 1523 Gustav Vasa was crowned king of an independent state which included Scania. The influence of the German Reformation started by Luther at the beginning of the sixteenth century quickly spread to Denmark, and in 1536 Lutheranism was established as the state religion, with the king as its head.

Christian IV: 'the architect king' 1588–1648

Danish architectural history properly starts with the very long reign of Christian IV, the 'architect king' (born 1577, reigned 1588–1648). Under his leadership, Danish international trade flourished: the East India Company was established and the small territory of Tranquebar in India colonised. In the first twenty years of his reign he started to transform Copenhagen into a royal capital, creating the harbours and provision yards 2 south of the Slot and commissioning the building of the Exchange 7. He designed, had built and rebuilt the royal summer palace of Rosenborg 3, and Holmens Church 6 was started. A transformation of the open space, now Kongens Nytorv, into an octagonal monumental square was planned but not executed. On the island of Amager the new town of Christianshavn 5 was established, one of twenty such new cities that Christian set up throughout the kingdom. The king followed architectural and urban models of the Dutch Renaissance: the

Copenhagen in 1660

modestly sized buildings are of red brick, occasionally articulated with bands of sandstone, and their architects, such as Hans van Steenwinckel the Younger, were quite often from Holland. The rectangular layout of Christianshavn around its canals and surrounded by a crescent of neat brick fortifications is also characteristically Dutch. The scant evidence of the domestic architecture of the period survives in the houses in Amagertorv 4 and at Strandgade in Christianshavn 5.

Christian's building programme was interrupted in 1625 by Denmark's involvement in the Thirty Years War, when the king unsuccessfully led the Protestant Union against a Catholic alliance of German states. His armies were defeated in 1629, and an impoverished Denmark lost the southern half of the Jutland peninsula. The few buildings of the period after this catastrophe include the remarkable Nyboder quarter of 1631 8, built to house shipyard workers; and the last building commissioned by the king, Steenwinckel the Younger's Trinitatis Church 9, with its humanistically inspired combination of church, university library and astronomical observatory. Towards the end of his reign Christian presided over naval and military defeats at the hands of Holland and Sweden, and in the peace of 1645 Denmark was forced to cede further large portions of its territory.

Baroque and Rococo 1649–1759

In the early years of the reign of Christian's successor Frederik III (1648–70), Denmark lost a further third of its territory in wars, and in 1659 it was compelled to cede the area east of the Øresund, Skåne, to Sweden. In a country made nearly bankrupt by war there was little architectural activity, and that which remains from Frederik's reign is restricted to the wooden fittings of Holmens Church **6**. In 1660 a new constitution was framed which, modelled on France's absolute monarchy, considerably reduced the powers of nobles and landowners, and enhanced those of the king. The new court, now no longer peripatetic but centred in Copenhagen, required the service of large numbers of officials, and between 1660 and about 1700 the population of the city grew from about 30,000 to about 60,000. The king patronised another Dutchman, Henrik Rüse, to design the Citadellet **11**, which was started in 1662 to reinforce Christian IV's circuit of walls at its northern end where it met the sea.

Frederik's successor, Christian V (1670–99), in 1688 regularised an existing patch of open ground on the edge of the city to provide Copenhagen's first large and formally organised public open space: Kongens Nytorv ('King's New Square'), laid out in a Baroque oval with the fine equestrian statue of the king by French sculptors at its centre. Copenhagen's first Baroque palace, Charlottenborg **13**, constructed on its east side, brought southern European sobriety to the new square.

The major buildings of Frederik IV's reign (1699–1730) included the country palace of Frederiksberg Slot **18**, the remarkable 'Røde Kancellibygning' or Chancellery of 1715–20 **21** and the Opera House **20**. His reign was also marked by catastrophes: in 1711 a plague which had originated in Constantinople struck Copenhagen and reduced its population of about 65,000 by a third, and in 1728 a fire destroyed more than half the old city together with the University Library housed in the Trinitatis Church **9**.

Under Christian VI (1730–46), who was influenced by German Pietism, all forms of public entertainment were discouraged but education became

Houses Græbrødretorv 1–7

Houses Fiolstræde 18

valued, and in the 1730s, Europe's first essay at universal education was attempted. From 1733 to 1745 the king rebuilt the Slot, although this had not been damaged in the fire of 1728. This grandiose new royal palace, unimaginatively named Christiansborg and designed by the master builder Elias David Häusser, had interiors which introduced both the French Rococo and Viennese Baroque to Copenhagen. While the palace itself later burned down in 1794, the delicate Riding School and Marble Bridge **24** to the west survive. Their architect was Niels (Nicolai) Eigtved (1701–54), who had trained in Italy and with Pöppelmann in Dresden, Germany, and who at the same time also designed the crown prince's palace **27** across the canal to the west of the Slot. In the rebuilding of the city after the fire, timber-framed houses were still permitted, and some examples of the domestic architecture of the period survive at Magstæde **10**, Gråbrødretorv, Fiolstræde and Gammel Mønt. Towards the end of the king's reign, in 1742, the Royal Dockyards which since the 1600s had remained on their site south of the Slot were abandoned and extensive new yards established on the island of Holmen **26**.

The year 1748 was the tercentenary of the establishment of the royal house of Oldenburg, and in 1746 Frederik V (1746–66) commissioned Eigtved to design a circular church to celebrate the occasion. It was to be sited on vacant land to the north of Kongens Nytorv. The development was taken as an opportunity to establish Copenhagen as a serious competitor with other

Introduction

more southerly European cities, for example Nancy enhanced by the extensions of 1705–63, and the plans were soon augmented to include a substantial extension to the city on land to the east of the church. The new district's
streets were to be lined with small regular palaces, and it was named
Frederiksstaden **29** after the king. In the centre Eigtved laid out a large
octagonal space, Amalienborg, and for its four diagonal sides designed near-
identical palaces, one for each of four of the king's ministers. An equestrian
statue of the king was to be placed at its centre. Roads on a rectangular
layout surrounded this square, and these were to be lined with smaller
palaces. While the circular church remained incomplete until 1894, the
ensemble was finished to the original plan and remains one of the most
remarkable examples of eighteenth-century Late Baroque urbanism in Europe.
In 1751 Eigtved was appointed the first director of the Copenhagen Academy
of Arts but he held the post for only three years before an early death in
1754. His death marked the end of the influence at the court of German
Rococo, and from then on more classical French models were adopted.
Laurids de Thurah, master of the French manner and Eigtved's contemporary
and rival, succeeded him as court architect, but only lived another four years.

Classicism 1760–1798

Denmark's economy and trade prospered during the second half of the
eighteenth century but in Copenhagen the monarchy started no new building
works apart from the Sølvgades Kaserne (barracks) **33** of 1765–71. Towards
the end of the century Denmark remained neutral during the American War of
Independence and continued to trade with all the participants. Domestic
changes included the reform of the system of rural landholding in which much
of the agricultural land formerly held by large owners was compulsorily sold
to the peasants who became freeholders, the pattern which more or less
survives to this day. In 1794 a fire destroyed the royal palace, Christiansborg
Slot, and the royal family moved into one of the palaces in Amalienborg
where its successors still live. In the following year another more extensive
fire destroyed almost a quarter of the city. It was quickly rebuilt to a more
regular pattern with wider streets, and new regular blocks of houses of grey-
or white-painted masonry were erected. The blocks had chamfered corners
to allow for the easy access of fire-fighting equipment. Several fine aristo-
cratic houses survive from this time, including on Kongens Nytorv **35** that of
the architect Caspar Frederik Harsdorff (1735–99) who had been a pupil of
Eigtved, and Erichsens Palæ **40**, also designed by Harsdorff. While best
known for the very severely classical royal chapel in Roskilde Cathedral

(see Excursions), Harsdorff also designed the more delicate Screen **38** across Amaliegade which now provides the entrance from that street to Amalienborg Plads.

Neoclassicism 1799–1847

In the Napoleonic wars Denmark failed to ally itself with either Britain or France, becoming an enemy of both, and in 1801 the entire Danish fleet was surrendered to the British navy under Nelson in the Battle of Copenhagen. While this constituted a crushing defeat, the event—together with the influence of the Romantic movement in Germany—served to fuel an emerging Danish nationalism evidence of which started to appear in a new interest in Nordic literature and a new Danish poetry. In 1807 the British fleet, attempting to persuade Denmark to ally itself with the forces fighting Napoleon, used Congreve rockets to bombard Copenhagen and the city and its inhabitants became the first civilian targets of such bombing. Much of the centre of the city including the Cathedral and the area around the university was damaged in the fires lit by the rockets.

The settlement which ended the Napoleonic wars required Denmark to surrender Norway. The annexation of this country to Sweden in 1814 further encouraged Danish nationalism, and demands began to be made for the reform of the constitution and an end to the absolute monarchy. In the same year a Schools Act, the first of its kind in Europe, established compulsory education for all 7- to 14-year-olds. Much of the centre of Copenhagen which had been rebuilt after the fire only twenty years earlier had to be reconstructed, but now the programme included some important public buildings. The architect for many of these was Christian Frederik Hansen (1756–1845), who had been Harsdorff's pupil at the Academy and had first practised in Holstein and around Hamburg. Later, as chief architect to the Danish state, Hansen brought to the buildings he was asked to design a severe and delirious Romantic Classicism heavily influenced by the French revolutionary architects E.-L. Boullée and C. N. Ledoux. His debut, the Law Courts and prison on Nytorv of 1805–15 **47**, was followed by a new church for Christiansborg Slot **53**, one of whose wings it now constitutes, the reconstruction of the Cathedral, and the nearby Soldins Stiftelse **51** and the former Metropolitan School **49**. Danish intellectual life flowered in the 1810s and 1820s. The Romantic innovations of Hansen were matched both by artists such as the painters Christen Købke and Christoffer Wilhelm Eckersberg and the sculptor Bertel Thorvaldsen, and by writers and scientists such as Rasmus Rusk and H. C. Ørsted.

Introduction

In 1834, responding to pressure, the king (Frederik VI 1803–39) established four consultative assemblies, none of them in Copenhagen, and thereby began the process of dismantling the absolute monarchy which was only to be completed in 1901. Copenhagen's final monument to the eras of Romanticism and of absolutism, Thorvaldsens Museum **55** of 1839–48, was designed by the then youngish architect Michael Gottlieb Birkner Bindesbøll (1800–56) who had travelled widely, was familiar with Schinkel's work and who went on to design the first buildings of the more democratic Denmark of the 1850s, for example the Medical Association housing **56** and the Agricultural College at Frederiksberg **60**.

Industrialisation and its problems came very late to Denmark whose economy during the first half of the nineteenth century depended on successful and efficient small-scale farming (which produced grain for export mainly to Britain), international trade; and small-scale manufacturing in Copenhagen. The population of the capital which at the beginning of the century had been about 100,000 continued to grow slowly. In the 1840s, the movement for universal education was furthered by the establishment of 'folk high schools' at the urging of N. F. S. Grundtvig (1783–1872), educational reformer and theorist. In this programme, which had no parallel in the rest of Europe, teachers were encouraged to live with groups of their pupils, and the ethos included a strong inclination to nationalism, the rediscovery of Denmark's Nordic traditions and an appreciation of the crafts.

Eclecticism 1848–1914

A new king, Frederik VII, came to the throne in 1848, an unfortunate year for the monarchy: Europe was torn with revolution and riot and demands for more democratic forms of government. Denmark was not excepted and the king voluntarily ended the absolute monarchy and instituted constitutional reforms. Two parliamentary chambers were established with suffrage to all men of 30 and older, and the powers of the parliament separated from those of the judiciary. The king continued, however, to head a cabinet of his own choosing.

In 1850 in a Copenhagen freed from its constraints as a fortified royal city, a start was made on demolishing the ramparts, and development outside them was allowed for the first time. The sites of the ramparts themselves were developed as the wide string of parks and gardens which now stretch almost continuously from the south-west where in 1853 the

Tivoli pleasure gardens **57** were one of the first uses to be established outside the walls, to the Kastellet in the north-east. Parts of the former moat remained as small lakes within the parks while between these and immediately outside very large blocks of flats for the middle classes were built, modelled on Parisian patterns, for example **63**. Copenhagen and its industries expanded and prospered, and cheap housing was built for their workers. The non-domestic buildings of the 1850s and 1860s exhibit tough structures with tough eclectic decoration and include Herholdt's University Library **58** and Grøns Pakhus (warehouse), and Christian Hansen's Municipal Hospital of 1859–63 **59** and Zoological Museum.

In 1863 the last king of the Oldenburg dynasty, Frederik VII, died. In the following year his successor was immediately involved with Prussia in a brief war about the position of the border between the two countries across the Jutland peninsula. At the conclusion of the war a new border was established near Kolding, about 60 kilometres north of its present position, and over the following forty years many Danish-speakers from the lost Danish territories emigrated to the United States. This loss, however, encouraged those farmers who remained to the north to organise themselves, and in 1882 the first co-operative farming enterprise was set up. Danish agriculture flourished, first in cereals and dairy products, later in meat.

In Copenhagen, which remained Denmark's only large city, more and more industries were set up. To house the new urban workers, in the 1870s the first philanthropic housing association was established, with its first buildings **61**, at Øster Søgade, designed by Frederik Bøttger who went on in the 1890s to build the 'Kartoffelrœkkerne' terraces **70** in Østerbro. Meanwhile, Copenhagen's stock of public and commercial buildings was being augmented with, in a festival of eclecticism, the new Royal Theatre **62** of 1872–74 designed with Ove Petersen by the erratic Vilhelm Dahlerup who also contributed the charming pantomime theatre in the Tivoli Gardens, and the first brewery for Carlsberg **64**. In 1874 work on the Marble Church **34** at Frederiksstaden which had been abandoned in 1770 was finally restarted, and the completion in 1894 of its elegant dome provided the city with a new landmark. In 1884 Christiansborg Slot which then housed the Royal Museum, art collections and library was destroyed in another fire. To house the displaced functions new buildings were erected including the uninspired National Museum of Art 1889–96 **69**, and the library on the site of one of Christian IV's harbours.

Introduction

The land of the former ramparts also provided a site for one of Copenhagen's triumphant but few examples of 'National Romanticism', the Town Hall **71**, for the design of which a competition—won by Martin Nyrop—was held in 1892. Another large example is the Klint father and son's extraordinary memorial church **95** to Grundtvig, although this was started twenty years later. The pan-European spread of Art Nouveau at the turn of the century left scarcely any mark in Denmark, and the villas and commercial buildings of Anton Rosen (1859–1928) often suggest a continuing nineteenth-century eclecticism of local inspiration rather than an awareness of international architectural currents.

In the fifty years between 1850 and 1900, Copenhagen's population had grown from 150,000 to about half a million people (about the same as today's), many of them still housed in crowded and insanitary conditions. The beginning of the new century was marked in 1901 by the final extinction of monarchical power and the establishment in its place of a constitutional monarchy and full parliamentary government, although full adult suffrage for those over 25 only followed in 1915.

Nordic classicism 1915–1928

Denmark remained neutral in the First World War and its trade prospered. As part of the settlement of the war, after a plebiscite held to determine the position of the country's border with Germany, the frontier was established across the narrowest part of the Jutland peninsula where it remains. In 1924, the Danish people elected their first social democratic government, and have continued to do so ever since.

In the period from about 1915 to 1930, much of Nordic architecture took a different turn from that pursued in the more southerly European countries. The earlier development of a nationalistic, romantic, folkloristic and craft-derived architecture was abandoned. It was replaced by a 'Nordic classicism', exemplified in Sweden in the work of Gunnar Asplund and Sigurd Lewerentz, and in Finland by that of Alvar Aalto. This movement was championed in Denmark by the art historian Vilhelm Wanscher and the architect Carl Petersen, who, working with Hans Henrik Koch, designed the little museum at Fåborg on the island of Fyn, 1912–15. In Copenhagen the larger examples of this Neoclassicism include domestic buildings, financed by the state with money made available under legislation for the promotion of social housing dating from 1915. Povl Baumann's block at Tavsensgade **92**, 1919–20, and

Hornbækhus **96**

the early work of Kay Fisker (1893–1965) such as the very severe flats at Hornbækhus **96**, in their spareness and objectivity and almost complete lack of classical ornament, both achieve the timeless quality of true classicism. At the same time, these large blocks were complemented by more modestly scaled schemes such as Henningsen and Bentsen's at Bellahøj **94** of 1921 which consist entirely of rows of cottages whose cosy forms derive from ideas of the garden city, but whose layout is as ruthlessly rectilinear as that of the Nyboder quarter of two centuries earlier. Alternatives to rows did, however, get built, inspired by the theories of Parker and Unwin and Camillo Sitte, and examples are to be found at Godthåbsvej **88**, sponsored by the Garden Home Association.

Schools such as that at Øregård of 1923–24 by Edvard Thomsen show how well Neoclassical planning devices such as the atrium suited the programme.

Introduction

The most striking and worrying example of the style in Copenhagen was supplied by Hack Kampmann and others' Police Headquarters **90** started in 1918, whose size and bald exterior alarmingly anticipate the architecture of a decade later in countries with fascist regimes.

International modernism 1929–1960

The prosperity of the early 1920s was followed by the effects of the international economic Depression from which Denmark was not protected. To counter its effects, in 1933 the state instituted a comprehensive system of social security, reforms in education and, of great consequence for Danish architects, the provision of housing and allotments. Much of the framework then established is still in place and this, together with the deliberate use of taxation to distribute wealth across the population of Denmark's scattered and varied territory, has earned the country its reputation for high taxes, but may also account for one of the highest standards of living in Europe.

The credit for the arrival of modern architecture in the Nordic countries is usually given to Asplund for his work at the Stockholm exhibition of 1930. While Asplund's temporary buildings were as much inspired by Russian Constructivism as by the early buildings of, for example, Le Corbusier or Mies van der Rohe, they acted as catalyst for the almost immediate adoption by many Nordic architects of the forms and language of European modernism. Two buildings in Copenhagen compete for modernism's debut: Bent Helweg-Møller's *moderne* newspaper offices for *Berlingske Tidende* **99** of 1928–30 and Fisker and Møller's flats **101** at Vodroffsvej, 1929. The latter's first design had Neoclassical façades which were restyled modern shortly before building began. The continuing and ambitious Danish state-sponsored housing programme of the 1930s meshed with the ambitions of modern architects. In particular, the severe very long straight lines and the general baldness of surface favoured by the German modernists found echoes in the traditions of Danish housing design, which included not only the immediately earlier Neoclassical schemes but which also reached back at least as far as the seventeenth century to Christian IV's Nyboder scheme **8**. All that was further required was to cut up closed housing blocks into strips so that all flats had good and equal access to air and light. Again, Fisker and Møller demonstrated the method in their Vester Søgade housing **110** of 1935–39 where a simple organisation is extended to a length of 320 metres (over 1,000 feet). This scheme is distinguished from its models in its use of materials: large areas of

unmodulated rendering are risky in the northern winters, and even if the
buildings had concrete frames modern architects were content to continue to
incorporate Danish brick as a facing material into the modern repertoire.

While some among the older generation of Danish architects such as
Fisker gracefully transferred their allegiance to modernism, it appeared
the only choice for the slightly younger generation who included Mogens
Lassen (1901–), and Arne Jacobsen (1902–71), both of whom subsequently produced distinguished work. The early work of Jacobsen, who
was later to become Denmark's most internationally celebrated modern
architect, included a housing scheme, the suburban Bella Vista **107** at
Klampenborg on the coast, started in 1931. In the later little block of
shops and offices **113** of 1937 in Gammeltorv in the heart of the old city,
Jacobsen demonstrated a distinctive and possibly Danish sensibility,
especially in the use of materials, largely independent of the 'International
Style' promoted by Hitchcock and Johnson.

When the Second World War broke out in 1939, Denmark attempted to
retain its neutrality, but in 1940 the country was invaded by German
troops en route for Norway. The ruling monarch Christian X was not
deposed, and the civilian government was only replaced by a German
administration in 1943. Danish agriculture remained productive and food
was never in short supply; Copenhagen was never shelled or bombed, and
the main hardships suffered by its population were the loss of liberty and the
persecution of minorities.

After the war Denmark became increasingly prosperous. It joined the North
Atlantic Treaty Organisation (NATO) in 1949, but retained a 'special relation-
ship' with the other Nordic countries and remained until 1974 a member of
the European Free Trade Association (EFTA). Changes to the Constitution in
1953 abolished parliament's upper house, permitted female succession to
the throne, and incorporated the huge territory of Greenland into Denmark as
a 'county'. In post-war Copenhagen, ambitious programmes were reinstituted
to replace worn-out and slum housing. The new developments were nearly all
in the suburbs, but were well served by a carefully planned and integrated
system of public transport, and were successfully landscaped with a zeal
unknown in more southerly countries. They followed models from the entire
range of those established all over Europe: from the towers in a park such as
Bellahøj **130** started in 1949, 'neighbourhoods' of mixed housing types, to the

Introduction

persisting Danish tradition of neatly or poetically arranged rows epito-
mised by the beautiful scheme by Poul Ernst Hoff and Bennet Windinge at
Søndergårdsparken **128** of 1949–50. All these were built in a range of
materials and forms which largely ignored the rendering and flat roofs of
modernism, and materials and forms more suitable to the Danish climate
were employed, including much brick and timber. Carefully maintained and
with their landscaping matured, these now present a calm benign image of
modern living; even the cars which in such developments elsewhere now tend
to overrun the ground do not appear too obtrusive.

Social democratic pluralism 1961–1998

It was too good to last. In the 1960s, as in many other European countries, the state decided to do what many influential architects recom-
mended: to modernise the building industry, and to replace the crafts by
industrialised methods. Earlier complex arrangements were replaced by
layouts which could be negotiated by the cranes which assembled the
heavy pre-cast self-finished concrete units which superseded earlier walls
made of brick or clad in timber. Architects were ready to supply diagrammatic 'collective' layouts in which the programme, which often included
schools, welfare buildings and shops, could be designed as an entity. The
most spectacular of these schemes, with its five very long very tall slabs,
at Høje Gladsaxe **146** of 1963–68, suffered ever since its completion from
the defects typical of systems of its kind and had to be reclad in 1990–92.
Completely different in approach were the schemes at Farum Midtpunkt **151**
1970–74, where the entire development was built on decks over car parking,
and at Albertslund **145** where the ground was carpeted with a warren of
2,000 lowish buildings. These too suffered from both social problems and
building defects and have subsequently been 'restored'. All these schemes
were built on open land. The state's idea of urban renewal was to demol-
ish large sections of Copenhagen's nineteenth-century working-class
suburbs and replace these with industrialised buildings and layouts, and
such a programme was started in the late 1960s in Nørrebro which is now
scarred by large crude 'panel-buildings' only marginally better than their
contemporaries in the former German Democratic Republic. After protests
similar to those in Amsterdam at the same time, this programme was
finally halted after massive demonstrations by an alliance of hippies, other
activists and squatters. The legacy of this movement can still be seen in
'Christiania', the squatted 'free city' on Christianshavn.

While during the decade 1965–75 the state promoted its deranged programmes of mass housing, other Danish architecture was becoming internationally celebrated for buildings demonstrating a regional sensibility of form
and materials and great sensitivity to their sites. These counter examples
included the atrium houses at Kingo (near Helsingør and beyond the scope of
this book) by Jørn Utzon and those at Usserød by Carl Frederiksen and
others, and the earlier phases of Jørgen Bo and Vilhelm Wohlert's lovely
Louisiana Museum **138**. Arne Jacobsen's designs had since about 1955
become, by contrast, increasingly aligned with the internationalism of his
North American contemporaries such as Skidmore Owings and Merrill, and
Eero and Eliel Saarinen: the Town Hall at Rødovre **136** of 1955 shows a
marked shift from that of the early 1940s at Søllerød **124**; the slab of the SAS
Royal Hotel **139** of 1960 in Copenhagen's centre remains the city's tallest
building after the Town Hall; and his National Bank **148** of 1965–78, while not
tall, could find itself anywhere in the world—only some of its 'Nordic' materials associate it with its location. The layout and buildings he designed for the
civic centre of Rødovre **136**, **150** demonstrate his ideas at its most benign: an
unlikely synthesis of the best of Copenhagen and Chicago.

Copenhagen's large new post-war suburbs of which the housing schemes
constituted the greater part were, even if of variable architectural quality
or sanity, carefully planned, often round or near existing 'village' nuclei,
and included public transport connections, schools, shops, libraries,
welfare buildings and churches. In particular, the lavish programmes and
budgets and the large sites which the state Lutheran Church furnished
provided opportunities for the exploration of forms and patterns of
organisation which could not be pursued in other building types, and some
architects like Johann Otto von Spreckelsen (1929–) at Farum **156** and
Inger and Johannes Exner (both born 1926) specialised in them as, for
example, at Præstebro **147**. One of the most notable works of Jørn
Utzon's very small œuvre is the church at Bagsværd **153**.

Since about the mid-1980s the architectural scene in Denmark has shown
two contradictory tendencies. The first is a continuing attempt by architects
to explore what seems to remain valuable in the Nordic tradition of modest
forms, usually simple boxes (although these may be surprisingly long) of
classical or vernacular origins, finished in modest or 'poor' local materials
and often capped with sensibly pitched and extraordinarily crisply detailed
roofs, all well adapted to a climate of extremes. The second is the usually

uncritical importing of up-to-date architectural fashions from anywhere in the world but often from North America. The many although often deliberately shaggily detailed housing schemes such as **157** and most recently at Egebjerggård **165** designed by Tegnestuen Vandkusten exemplify the first tendency. The work of, for example, KHR (Knud Holscher and others) has frequently typified the second. Dissing + Weitling, successors to Jacobsen, and Henning Larsen's office pursue a course somewhere in between as in the latter's work at the former Tuborg Brewery site in Hellerup **182** and in the new galleries at the Ny Carlsberg Glyptotek **72**. The late twentieth-century avant-garde is represented by Søren Robert Lund's Ark **184** at Ishøj, and Schmidt, Hammer & Lassen's extension to the Royal Library **180** started in 1995, neither of which possess any specifically 'Danish' features and, apart from the latter's Nordic granite cladding, either of which could be anywhere. Examples of the gamut of Danish housing design of the last fifteen years, usefully placed side-by-side, can be inspected in the bizarre experimental housing quarter at Egebjerggård, Ballerup **165**.

The present queen Margrethe II has been monarch since 1972, and in that year and following a referendum Denmark became a full member of the European Economic Community, and subsequently, although with reservations about monetary union, of the European Union. At the time of writing, Copenhagen is a smallish European city most of whose population of about 470,000 (in the city proper) are successfully employed in trade, banking, services and public administration. The new bridge and tunnel **185** which will carry road and rail traffic across and under the Sound will connect southern Europe with Sweden, not only allowing the remarkable possibility of through trains from London to Stockholm, but ensuring that Copenhagen will continue to command the Sound.

Christiansborg, courtyard: 1, 81

Foundations 1167

1Ak **Ruins of Bishop Absalon's castle** 1167

Prins Jørgens Gård 1, Christiansborg (entrance to the right of main gate facing Christiansborg Slotsplads)

In the 1160s, Bishop Absalon of Roskilde received the town of Copenhagen from his foster-brother King Valdemar the Great and built a small commanding and defensive castle on slightly elevated land on a small island. The site of his castle remained the seat of power in Copenhagen until 1731. Although successive rebuildings in the intervening years destroyed much of the centre of Absalon's castle, its remains were fully excavated when the present Christiansborg **81** (illustration opposite) was started in 1906, and these were arranged for public display in 1974–79. The castle consisted of a circle of fine white limestone walls to which projecting square towers were later added, and parts of its lower courses and the remains of some of the buildings originally within can be seen. When Copenhagen was attacked during the wars in the fourteenth century, in 1369 the upper parts of the walls were demolished by a team of masons from Lübeck. Later a second castle was built and this, much extended and altered, remained the royal residence until it was rebuilt by Christian VI in 1731–32. Parts of the foundations of the walls of this second castle are just discernible.

Rosenborg Slot 3 from Rosenborg Have

Christian IV: 'the architect king' 1588–1648

2Ao Proviantgården (Provision Yard), Tøjhus Museum ex **Tøjhus (Arsenal)** and **Bryggehus (brewery)** 1599–1605
Tøjhusgade

Christian IV's first work to equip Copenhagen for its emerging role as a major colonial and trading power was the transformation of the island on which the Slot stood into a naval dockyard. Begun in 1599, three long piers were constructed and between these two docks were excavated, one lying behind the Exchange **7** (on what is now Slotholmsgade), and a square one to the west. Both have subsequently been filled in, but the square shape of the latter's basin is preserved in the courtyard in front of the Royal Library. Of the original buildings, on the west side of the second dock the plain **Tøjhus**, the armoury, 160 metres (520 feet) long and completed in 1604, survives

Bryggehus

and is now used as a museum. To the west, the enormous eight-storey and hip-roofed **Bryggehus** (brewery), begun later and finished in 1618, supplied the navy's beer which provided a healthier alternative to the city's polluted drinking water. It was destroyed by fire in 1767 and rebuilt. It is now best seen from the west across Frederiksholm Kanal which originally provided its access.

3Ag Rosenborg Slot 1606–34
Øster Farimagsgade/Rosenborg Have

 Nørreport

The official royal residence was the ramshackle medieval Slot or castle in the centre of the city. Christian IV designed and had built this small fortified and moated palace as a summer and retirement residence standing in its own grounds outside the walls, but easily reached on horseback from the Slot. Here he could indulge his hobby of architecture unhampered: its original design, of 1606, was a plain rectangular box of brick with simple decoration in Gotland sandstone. The king later added the three square towers—one on the west side and two on the east, all finished in 1633—which now give the building its picturesque silhouette, their style influenced by the architecture of the Dutch Renaissance. On the ground floor, the king's suite of

Christian IV: 'the architect king'

rooms has been restored to an approximation of its original state with fine panelling and ceilings. The grand salon on the first floor was restyled in the eighteenth century when the present copper roof was also added. The building was restored in 1866 and again in 1996.

☞ Kronprinsessegade, the road on the south-eastern side of Rosenborg Have, the pleasant and well-used park in which the palace now stands, is lined with the Neoclassical Meyns Pavilloner **44**. Sølvgades Kaserne **33** and the Statens Museum for Kunst **69** both lie to the north.

4Ak House 1616
Amagertorv 6

This is the earliest house of which parts have survived the various catastrophes which destroyed successive generations of Copenhagen's housing stock. It was built for Mathias Hansen, a mayor of the city, of brick with stone trim in lavishly decorated twin-gabled Dutch style. As the inscription on the right-hand gable records, the façade was completely rebuilt in 1898.

5Ap Christianshavn begun 1617
[Islandsbrygge]

Earlier in his reign, Christian IV had started to equip the state with the naval harbours and the Provision Yard and Arsenal **2**. While these were being finished, immediately to the south of the Slot he started this new township and civil and commercial harbour, the largest of his projects in Copenhagen. Dutch engineers were employed to lay it out, partly on reclaimed land, with a neat rectangular grid of canals and streets set inside a defensive semi-circle of moated fortifications facing Amager. The earlier wide neck of water between Copenhagen and the island of Amager was narrowed to the

Christianshavns Kanal

size of a small river. A remnant perhaps of the area's Dutch origins, some of the warehouses such as Overgaden neden Vandet 45–47 are still equipped with Dutch 'hijsbalken', the lifting hooks still common on houses in Holland.

Unlike the centre of Copenhagen proper, the district never suffered from fire or bombing and it retains much of its original scale and some of its original fabric. The earliest house now remaining, of 1626, is at Strandgade 28, plain and of two storeys. Next to it, numbers 30 and 32, of 1624–36, were originally a pair, but number 30 has had its gable simplified and number 32 has lost its gable completely and had a second floor added. On the opposite corner, across Torvegade, is the grand number 14, illustrated right, each of its two tall four-storey façades topped with a pediment. The stone façade of number 6 conceals a half-timbered courtyard.

Of non-domestic buildings several fine warehouses remain, including Eigtveds Pakhus, now part of the Ministry of Foreign Affairs 159, and that of 1882 at Gammel Dok half way along Strandgade. The former Naval Hospital at Overgaden oven Vandet was converted to house the Royal Danish Naval Museum. Well after the establishment of Christianshavn two churches were built: Vor Frelsers Kirke (Our Saviour's Church) 15 of 1682–96; and in the following century Christianskirken 31 of 1755–59.

In an exemplary programme of urban renewal, the infrastructure of the district was spruced up in the 1990s, and many houses and the sometimes very large former warehouses have been tactfully restored and converted. The area also houses a later township, the hippie squatter enclave of Christiania, its entrance off Prinsessegade. The area around Christianskirken is being redeveloped with large but undistinguished blocks of flats. The most recent architecturally noteworthy addition to the area's stock is the Arkitekternes Hus 181 in front of Gammel Dok at Strandgade 27.

6Ak **Holmens Kirke** 1619, 1641–43, 1705–08
Holmens Kanal
Chapel 1705–08: Johan Conrad Ernst

This brick building was originally a late sixteenth-century smithy. In 1619 Christian IV had it converted into a church for use by the navy. When the building was expanded in 1641–43 and the present arrangement established, only the gable of the earlier building which faces the canal was retained. The church has an irregular Greek-cross plan: the nave and the choir have three bays and the transepts two, and all have low segmental tunnel vaults with relief decoration in plaster. The white painted interior is fitted out with dark timber most of which is original having survived the successive Copenhagen fires. Pews completely fill the floor; galleries, which include a 'box' for the royal party in the choir, line nave and transepts; and the elaborate pulpit and altarpiece of 1640–42 are very finely carved. Added in 1705–08, the long (probably inaccessible) chapel to the south-east was designed by J. C. Ernst and contains the tombs of among others

the architects Christian Frederik Hansen and of Gustav Friedrich Hetsch, Hansen's son-in-law and a professor at the Academy.

Christian IV: 'the architect king'

7Ak **Børsen (Exchange)** 1619–20

Børs Gade

Lorenz van Steenwinckel and Hans van Steenwinckel the Younger

Christian IV actively encouraged Denmark's trade, and had this commodity exchange built. The 127 metre (419 feet) long two-storey building presents itself to the quay of the canal on the longest of the three piers which the king earlier had built out into the water from the Slot. (It therefore owes its elongated shape as much to its site as to any possible Danish preference for very long buildings.) The lower storey originally contained warehouses while the upper was fitted out as shops and offices reached by ramps at either end. The extraordinary central tower with its three intertwined dragons was based on a design by Ludwig Heidritter and completed in 1625. The Steenwinckels' original brick of the exterior was reclad in about 1860, and in 1902–06 the sandstone ornamentation was replaced.

8Ad **Housing, Nyboder** from 1631

Sankt Poulsgade 20–40 etc.

Østerport

Sankt Poulsgade 20–40

The 'architect king' provided Copenhagen with many new buildings for the institutions of the state, but here he created an entire new domestic quarter of 616 family houses for members of the services on a site within the walls but well away from the old city. The drastically simple layout and coherence characteristic of barracks and colonial settlements are reinforced by the present uniform yellow ochre colouring to the brushed-mortar brickwork. Long rows of what were originally single-storey cottages line the parallel streets, and between them lie small gardens. The quarter has been much altered: most of the terraces have had a second storey added and the only surviving original houses are now to be seen at Sankt Poulsgade 20–40. Number 20 was converted into a museum in 1931. The form of the estate may have had a strong influence on subsequent housing developments in Denmark many of which continue to demonstrate the persistence of the pattern of very long rows of houses.

Suensonsgade

☞ Old people's home and urban renewal **155**, Østerport Station **175**.

9Af Trinitatis Kirke og Rundetårn (Trinity Church and round tower) 1637–42 tower; 1637–56 church

Købmagergade/Landemærket

Hans van Steenwinckel the Younger

 Nørreport

This was the last project which Christian IV initiated in Copenhagen. Its programme which combines a church for the university, library and observatory suggests aspirations to cosmic significance characteristic of the Renaissance. While Steenwinckel is credited with the design, it is known that the king was also actively involved. The construction is of brick. The tall church, started by Christian but completed by his successor, combines nave and choir without transepts, and its design is firmly Gothic rather than classical. The University Library was housed in its roof. At the west end of the church Christian placed his squat almost featureless circular tower the roof of which, reached by a broad spiral ramp shallow enough for horses of the king's coach to climb, was to be used for astronomical observations.

The location of the library proved disastrous: in 1728 the church caught fire and the contents of the library were entirely destroyed. (Its replacement **58** was finally built in 1857–71.) The fittings of the church were also burnt, and the present arrangement dates from the 1730s; the finely carved Baroque altarpiece and pulpit are by Fridrich Ehbisch.

☞ Across Købmagergade to the west of the church and with entrances off Krystalgade and

Kannikestræde lies another of Christian's schemes, the **Regensen**, a student residence built in 1618–28. Still used by students, its rooms are arranged round a pleasant courtyard. Further to the west on the north side of Krystalgade at number 71 is the **Synagogue** of 1830–33 designed by Gustav Friedrich Hetsch. It was extended in 1885 and restored in 1958 by Henning Meyer.

10Aj Houses c. 1640

Magstræde 17–19

These modest houses from Christian IV's reign with their eminently combustible façades are rare survivals of the fire of 1728. They are now embedded in a street lined with masonry buildings constructed after the event.

Røde Kancellibygning, 'Red Chancellery' (1715–20), 21

Baroque and Rococo 1649–1759

1Ad Citadellet Frederikshavn, 'Kastellet' 1662–63

Henrik Rüse

Østerport

It was left to Christian IV's successor Frederik III to complete the new fortifications at their northern end where the city was most vulnerable to attack from the Sound. Designed by Rüse, a Dutch engineer, the small castle is a perfect example of a Baroque fortification, its plan a slightly irregular pentagon with a moat between inner and outer embankments. To the north and south are gates which are connected by a street lined with barracks. On the cross-axis, to the west of the parade ground at the centre, is the chapel of 1703–04 and to the east the Commander's house of 1725. The buildings are now occupied by offices for the army and its archive. The mill on the west side was built in 1847.

The Danish painter Christen Købke (1810–48) lived for much of his life in the castle where his father was the baker, and many of his paintings, some of which are in the Statens Museum for Kunst **69**, record its appearance then, in particular the striking deep red paint of the chunky woodwork of the gates and bridges.

☞ The church of St Alban's **68** is in the park to the south of the castle. The statue of **Den Lille Havfrue** (the 'Little Mermaid') is on the shore to the east of the Kastellet.

2Ak Kongens Nytorv 1680s

[Kongens Nytorv]

Christian IV had hoped to rid the space now occupied by Kongens Nytorv of its gallows, and reorder it to celebrate the absolute monarchy. It was his successor Christian V who began to realise the vision, when the present characteristically Baroque oval was first laid out. An equestrian statue of the king was placed at its centre. Its sculptors were the French Abraham César and Claude l'Amoureux, but the present statue is a copy. The most recent addition to the square is on the south-west corner: the metro station of 1996–98.

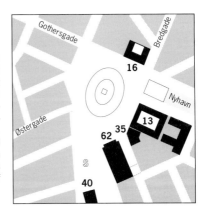

Baroque and Rococo

13Al Charlottenborg now **Royal Danish Academy of Fine Arts** 1672–77, 1683

Kongens Nytorv/Nyhavn

Evert Janssen (master builder)

[Kongens Nytorv]

The powerful politician Ulrik Frederik Gyldenløve, Stathalter (Governor) of Norway and illegitimate son of King Frederik III commissioned this palace. Its architectural significance lies in its size and in its unknown but probably Dutch designer's introduction of the Baroque balustrade and low-pitched hipped roof to Copenhagen. This replaced the decorated gable which had up to then been the symbol of power. Its siting was a fulfilment of Christian V's vision of Kongens Nytorv as a grand square surrounded by palaces. The original plan, completed in 1677 was U-shaped, but the U was closed in 1683 to form a rectangle enclosing the present courtyard. The final wing houses the grand Cupola Room which has a vaulted ceiling with sumptuous plaster decoration. The sober façade to Kongens Nytorv, of brick with sparing stone dressings, has projecting wings at the ends, while the centre is framed with a modest feature of giant Corinthian pilasters topped with a flat architrave over the entrance arch.

Since 1754 the building has housed the Royal Danish Academy of Fine Arts whose first principal was the architect Niels Eigtved.

14Al House 1681

Nyhavn 9

[Kongens Nytorv]

The canal Nyhavn ('new harbour') was commissioned by Frederik III to connect Kongens Nytorv to the sea. On its completion its quays were lined in Dutch style by merchants' houses of which this modest partially gabled example is the unique survival. Nyhavn became one of the city's red-light districts but in the 1970s an aggressive programme of gentrification produced the present picturesque but touristic nearly continuous row of restaurants along the north side.

5Ap **Vor Frelsers Kirke (Our Saviour's Church)**
1682–96, tower 1749–50

Sankt Annæ Gade, Christianshavn

Lambert van Haven

[Islandsbrygge]

Christianshavn's first church was started only
some sixty-five years after the foundation of the
township. (Its second was Christianskirken **31** of
the following century.) Its architect Van Haven
had travelled widely in Holland, France and Italy,
and brought his knowledge of up-to-date European Baroque to the job. The church has a
centralised Greek-cross plan developed by repeating a square module the size of one of the
corner bays. Set in from the undulating exterior
wall is a central bay marked at its corners by
Corinthian columns supporting the ceiling. The
whole is lit with very tall arched windows. The
handsome brick exterior elevations are ordered
on the module of the plan: each modular bay is
marked with a pair of Tuscan brick pilasters
which support the continuous sandstone architrave and frame a tall arched window. The lower
stages of the square tower are conventional
enough but these are crowned by the frivolous
gilded copper-covered steeple with its external
spiral stair, designed by Laurids de Thurah and
added in 1749–50. The architect admitted the
influence of the spire of Borromini's Sant' Ivo alla
Sapienza in Rome of 1642–60, although this is
much squatter; and locally he had the example of
the spiral dragons at the Exchange **7**.

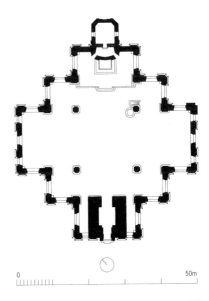

0   50m

Baroque and Rococo

16Ah Thotts Palæ now **French Embassy** 1683–86
Kongens Nytorv 4

[Kongens Nytorv]

The plan of the house was modelled on the French hotel particulier, but its original façade to Kongens Nytorv was remodelled in 1763–64 to the designs of Nicolas-Henri Jardin and its stucco decoration now forms an elegant counterpart to the brick of Charlottenborg **13** on the opposite corner.

17Af Reformert Kirke (Reformed Church)
1688–89

Gothersgade

Henrik Brockham

Nørreport

Lutheranism had been Denmark's state religion since the Reformation. Christian V, however, married a German Calvinist, Charlotte Amalie of Hessen-Kassel, and he introduced legislation allowing both Jews (from Portugal via Germany) and German Calvinists and French Huguenots to settle and have religious freedom in Copenhagen. The queen sponsored the building of this church for the latter two groups. It has a rectangular plan surmounted by a high hipped roof. The main axis is across the shorter dimension of the rectangle, and in an arrangement similar to that of Christianskirken **31** at Christianshavn the pulpit stands over the altar on this axis, and the three sides are lined with galleries. The treatment of the exterior is similar to that of the contemporary Vor Frelsers Kirke **15**: Ionic pilasters frame tall arched windows and, doubled, support a small pediment over the entrance.

18Be Frederiksberg Slot 1699–1703, 1733–38

Frederiksberg

Ernst Brandenburger, Laurids de Thurah, Elias David Häusser

Since 1869 the building, now painted a striking and characteristic 'Danish' yellow, has been occupied by the Danish Military Academy and the courtyard and interiors are inaccessible. The present ensemble is a result of a long building programme. The earliest part, the wing facing the grass steps leading to the park, was built 1699–1703 and commissioned as a small country palace by Frederik IV (reigned 1699–1730) when he was crown prince. Frederik wanted it modelled on an Italian villa, but this wing's plan has much in common with a Roman suburban palace such as the Palazzo Farnesina. Its elevations, however, have more in common with the urban Palazzo Farnese: it has regular bays with alternating angled and segmental hoods to the first-floor windows, and it only departs from the model in the unpleasantly bunched triple windows which mark the centre bay. Its architect may have been either the master builder Ernst Brandenburger or J. C. Ernst. The original wing had projecting pavilions at its ends, and these were extended outwards in 1708–09 by Johan Conrad Ernst to make a regular H-shaped plan. In 1733–38 the wings were extended to the south to enclose the courtyard, to Laurids de Thurah's

designs, and the gate house, by J. H. Koch, was added in 1829. The inaccessible interior houses a Baroque chapel of 1710 by W. F. Von Platen, and C. F. Harsdorff designed the dining room.

☞ The grounds, now a public park, were landscaped in the English style in the 1790s and their ornaments include the Apis Temple and the Chinese Pavilion **42**. Along Roskildevej to the west, its entrance at 59–61, is the **Søndermarkens Crematorium** of 1927–30. Its design, by Frits Schlegel and Edvard Thomsen, marks the transition between neoclassicism and the modernism of the same architects' later crematorium chapel at Mariebjerg **116**.

⏵Ak **Sankt Nicolai Kirke** c. 1690
Højbro Plads

The elaborate tall tower built at the end of the seventeenth century is the only part to remain of earlier churches on the site: it was repaired in 1915–17 with funds provided by Carl Jacobsen, the brewery magnate, when the body of the church was built to the designs of H. C. Amberg to replace that destroyed in the fire of 1795. Although in the 1530s the earlier church had been the setting for the first Lutheran sermon to be preached by ex-monk Hans Tavsen in Copenhagen and it thus became a focus for the Reformation in Denmark, the present building is no longer consecrated but used as a venue for exhibitions.

Baroque and Rococo

20Ah **Opera House** now **Østre Landsret (Eastern High Court)** 1701–02, extended 1902–03
Fredericiagade/Bredgade
Wilhelm Frederik von Platen (?), extension Martin Borch

[Kongens Nytorv]

An opera house of timber had existed in Amalienborg but it burnt down in 1689 and this sturdy brick building, perhaps designed by von Platen, was commissioned by Frederik IV as its replacement. Having housed the Danish parliament from 1884 to 1918, it is now used as the (eastern) High Court. It was originally a Dutch-inspired three-storey brick and hip-roofed box decorated on the exterior with giant pilasters enclosing panels of diapered brickwork. The entrance on Fredericiagade is marked with a pediment. In 1902–03, a tactful extension to the north was added in a 'corrected' version of the original. This was designed by Martin Borch and it is visible across the courtyard from Bredgade. If it were in England, its style would be characterised as 'Wrenaissance'.

☞ On the opposite side of Bredgade are the Medicinshistorisk Museum **37** (the former Academy of Surgeons), and a little further north the Kunstindustrimuseum **30**, the former Frederik's Hospital.

21Ao **Røde Kancellibygning ('Red Chancellery'** now **High Court)** 1715–20
Slotsholmsgade 4
Wilhelm Frederik von Platen and Johan Conrad Ernst (master builders)

The absolute monarchy required armies of administrators and Frederik IV provided this building to house a 'College' (later 'ministry') for them. Its site, behind the long Børsen, may have suggested its extremely elongated shape. Its three-storey elevation of fine brickwork is composed entirely of rows of windows which light the regularly arranged offices but which are spaced slightly too close together for classical taste. Those on the first floor are protected by the same alternating triangular and segmental hoods and stand on the same flat string course which its master builder J. C. Ernst used at Frederiksberg Slot **18**. The slightly projecting central seven bays are crowned with a huge segmental pediment (illustration page 30) containing the bust and the arms of King Frederik surrounded by military trophies.

3b **Fredensborg Palæ** 1720–24 etc.

Fredensborg, excursion from Humlebæk

Johan Cornelius Krieger and others

Fredensborg

The palace as it now stands together with the surrounding buildings form an unsatisfactory architectural composition, but the original building was one of Frederik IV's last contributions to the architecture of Copenhagen and its surroundings. It is still used as the royal family's summer residence. Designed by the landscape architect Krieger, the first residential building of 1720–24, which replaced an earlier hunting lodge, consisted of a stuccoed square two-storey block. At its centre stood a hall whose dome rose above the block. The original architecture was calm but unscholarly. In 1741 de Thurah added the four chimneys, one on each corner of the dome. In 1753 Eigtved contributed the four hip-roofed pavilions without balustrades which collide with each corner of the block. The octagonal courtyard and handsome gatehouses were designed by Harsdorff in 1774–76 when he also refaced the front of the original building. A second, rectangular, courtyard to the east houses the chapel. The interior includes the Kuppelsal (or central hall), and the room to the garden decorated in Rococo taste. The fine barrel-vaulted chapel contains an altarpiece, pulpit and font in magnificent Baroque by Friedrich Ehbisch. The garden was laid out in its present form by Nicolas-Henri Jardin in 1759–69.

3Ak **House for the Court Confectioner** 1732

Nybrogade 12

Philip de Lange

After the fire of 1728 timber buildings were banned, and this, by the Dutch architect de Lange, is a charming example of the decorated masonry constructions which followed, and a contrast to his later and more muscular Arsenal **26**.

Baroque and Rococo

24Ak **Christiansborg Palæ, Stables and Marble Bridge** 1733–45

Fredriksholms Kanal

Elias David Häusser

Towards the end of his reign Frederik IV had started to modernise the medieval royal palace on this site, the Slot. His successor Christian VI, however, abandoned the improvements and had a completely new and enormous palace built to the designs of the master builder Elias David Häusser. Drawings of this building suggest that it was no masterpiece, but the interiors supplied by the rivals Eigtved and de Thurah introduced French Rococo and Viennese Baroque to Copenhagen. Eigtved also designed the western

entrance to the palace's grounds, the suave Marble Bridge completed in 1745 and its two elegant and exuberantly decorated gatehouses which clearly show the influence of Pöppelmann, one of his German masters. The two curved wings which enclose the former riding ground and connect the gate to the palace are all that survive of Häusser's work.

The main palace was destroyed by fire in 1794 although the bridge survived, and C. F. Hansen was commissioned to design its replacement. Most of this too burnt down in 1884 and only the Slotskirke to the north **53** survived. Its successor, the present Christiansborg Slot which was rebuilt as a royal residence but which now houses Denmark's parliament, is described at **81**.

25Bc **Eremitagen** 1734–36

Jægersborg Dyrehave, Klampenborg

Laurids de Thurah

Ⓢ Klampenborg

This royal hunting lodge, sited on a slight eminence in the middle of the Dyrehave (deer park), was commissioned by Christian VI from the very young de Thurah well before the latter became court architect. Its plan is Palladian: the large dining room, its interior designed by de Thurah, is reached from the entrance via a vestibule and smaller rooms to the sides are connected *en suite*. Eigtved was commissioned to decorate the royal bedrooms and his Rococo contrasts with de Thurah's heavier Baroque.

The composition of the stuccoed elevations is highly unusual: while the ground floor is treated with a Neoclassical severity, the first floor is richly decorated, the wings on the entrance face crowned with segmental pediments. The whole composition is surmounted and unified by the huge mansard roof.

5Bf **Royal Dockyards** 1742–72

Holmen

A new dockyard to replace Christian IV's crowded and inadequate harbour south of Christiansborg Slot was established in the eighteenth century on three new linked 'islands' built in the harbour north of Christianshavn. Much of the site continued to be used by the navy until 1991. The central island, Holmen, was opened up to civilian use in 1995 and Copenhagen's architecture school now occupies a group of former workshops on Danneskolde Samsøes Allé. Most of the buildings were merely utilitarian, but in the 1740s the master builder Philip de Lange provided the designs for several with important symbolic functions. On the southernmost island, Arsenalø, the Arsenal was built in 1741 in the form of two blocks connected by a gated screen. The Guard House, built in 1742–43, is a one-and-a-half storey house with a pantiled mansard roof from

which emerges a tower incorporating a lookout and topped by the royal crown. The crane to the south was added in 1748–51. The lower parts of its timber structure are concealed inside a brick tower. Both these (inaccessible in 1997) are visible from across the water from the promenade at Amaliehaven.

7An **Prinsenspalæ** now **National Museum** 1743–44

Frederiksholm Kanal

Niels Eigtved

The original palace built for the crown prince, later Frederik V, faces Frederiksholm Kanal and the Stables of the Slot. It was subsequently extended to occupy the entire block between Stormgade and Vester Voldgade. Eigtved's design is modelled on the Parisian *hotel particulier*: three plain three-storey wings are arranged in a broad 'U' facing the canal, enclosing a courtyard and closed by a single-storey garden wing. The building was never burnt and still contains original interiors, some designed by Eigtved, which have been incorporated into and are accessible from the present National Museum. These provide a picture of how Haüsser's now vanished Slot 1 was furnished.

The palace was acquired for the Royal Museum of Nordic Antiquities in 1807 when it was first

extended to house and consolidated various scattered collections. It became the National Museum in 1892, and was remodelled in the 1930s. The rooms to the west were reordered around a new atrium in 1991–92 when a new entrance from Ny Vestergade was arranged and the former courtyard in the block to the west was filled in to provide space for temporary exhibitions. The architects for this work were Bornebusch Tegnestue working with various designers for the new installations.

8Bb **Frederiksdal (Pleasure Pavilion)** 1744–45

Frederiksdal, Furesø

Niels Eigtved (mansard 1752–53, J. G. Rosenberg)

Glimpses of this little Rococo building can be had only from one of the paths in the wood to the east of the road skirting the lake, and it is included to complete Eigtved's œuvre. Its plan is a simple rectangle with two small projections on the garden side. In 1752–53 the roof was altered and the present steep mansard was added by J. G. Rosenberg.

☞ Nicolai Abildgård's summer house **45** of 1805 is nearby to the north in Spurveskjul, and Sophienholm **43** is to the south.

Baroque and Rococo

29Ah   Frederiksstaden 1749–57

Niels Eigtved

[Kongens Nytorv]

Frederik V came to the throne in 1746. The following year marked the 300th anniversary of the establishment of the Oldenburg dynasty and he set about celebrating this and commemorating himself by commissioning a domed church to be built of marble. As architect to the court Eigtved was commissioned to design it, but enlarging his brief he proposed an entirely new urban quarter north of the existing city. The site was a parallelogram bounded by Toldbodgade to the north, Sankt Annæ Plads to the south, Bredgade to the west and the shore to the east. This was subdivided by two roads, Amaliegade running north–south, and at right angles to this Frederiksgade which was to be made the more important axis by a new church at its western end. At the intersection of the roads Eigtved placed a grand octagonal open space, Amalienborg Plads. This was established as an absolute monarchy's *place royale* after the king's death when the fine equestrian statue of the king by Jacques-François-Joseph Saly was finally placed in its centre in 1771.

The rest of the site was laid out with an irregular rectangular grid of streets. Palaces, one for each of four influential ministers, were planned on opposite corners of the octagon, while the lesser streets were to be lined with small palaces and houses the design of whose elevations were to be controlled by Eigtved. While much of the architecture was carried out in Eigtved's preferred light Rococo style, the ensemble is one of the most important and successful examples of Baroque urban planning in Europe and ranks with Bernini's Colonnade in front of St Peter's, Rome, of 1665–67, and the sequence of place Stanislaus, place Carrière and the hemicycle at Nancy of 1752.

The four palaces were not all started at the same time, and their interiors were subsequently refitted, but they share a common composition of a three-storey block of thirteen bays, its centre marked by a projecting giant order of coupled columns on a rusticated base, and topped with urns and the flourishing heraldic ornaments of the owner. Later, two-storey wings with gates were attached at an angle to the main block, and these returned at right angles along the streets which led into the octagon. The palace on the south-west side was designed by Eigtved for Minister Moltke, and built 1751–54. Its interiors are occasionally accessible.

After the fire of 1794 at Christiansborg, all four palaces were bought by the royal family and the southerly two used by the king and crown prince. Harsdorff's screen across Amaliegade **38** was built to connect them. The palace on the south-east, originally Brockdorf's, was completely re-built in 1828. The Marble Church **34** was started in 1770. The paving to the octagon was carried out in Italian marble in 1886.

The streets around Amalienborg Plads contain many large houses and small palaces both from the original foundation of Frederiksstaden and built subsequently. Amaliegade south of the octagon is lined on its west side with many fine examples built to Eigtved's rules. A pair were

designed by him at numbers 15–17, and de Thurah designed and built number 25 for himself.

Outstanding mansions remain on the east side of **Bredgade** ('Broad Street') at numbers 26, 34, 40–42, 46 and **Dehns Palæ** at number 54, of 1755 by Johann Gottfried Rosenberg, now owned by Danmarks Apotekerforening (The Danish Pharmaceutical Association) and inaccessible. The street also contains the former Frederik's Hospital, now the Kunstindustrimuseum **30**, and at

number 28 the former Berckentins Palæ, now **Odd Fellow Palæ** by Eigtved of 1755. Nineteenth-century developments include the sturdy Italianate block of **shops and flats** at number 63 of 1886–87 by Ferdinand Jensen.

☞ The harbour shore alongside Frederiksstaden was tidied up in 1983 to form Amaliehaven park and promenade. To the north are the Blue, Yellow and Vestindisk Warehouses **36** of the 1770s and 1780s.

30Ad **Kunstindustrimuseum (Museum of Decorative and Applied Arts) ex Frederik's Hospital** 1752, 1757

Bredgade 68

Niels Eigtved, Laurids de Thurah

 Østerport

The plans for Frederikstad included this hospital. The modest single-storey buildings surrounding the rectangular courtyard were designed by Eigtved while the pavilions flanking it on Bredgade were provided by de Thurah in 1757. The setting-out of the courtyard buildings provides an early example of modular planning: a single bay the size of the room containing a bed is regularly repeated round its sides. The hospital was closed in 1919 since when the buildings have housed the present museum.

☞ The Medicinshistorisk Museum **37** (the former Academy of Surgeons) is a little to the south of Bredgade and opposite it is the former Opera House **20**.

Baroque and Rococo

31Ap **Christianskirken** 1755–59
Strandgade, Christianshavn
Niels Eigtved, Georg David Anthon

[Islandsbrygge]

The Reformert Kirke (Reformed Church) **17** had
provided a place of worship for, among others,
German Calvinists. This church was built with
funds from the first Danish national lottery for
German-speaking Lutherans. The design was
prepared by Eigtved who died in 1754 before
work could be started, and building was continued by his son-in-law G. D. Anthon who also
designed the tower. Like the Reformed Church,
its plan is a rectangle with the main axis across
its short side. Three sides of the rectangle are
lined with three levels of galleries subdivided into
'boxes' like a theatre, and a royal box is provided
on the axis over the entrance. In a highly unusual
arrangement, the organ and pulpit are placed
above the altar. The disadvantage of the whole
arrangement is that light can only be provided
through the tall windows in the wall against which
the altar stands, causing glare for the congrega-
tion, and through the very small clerestory windows above the galleries.

32Ap **Orlogsmuseet** ex **Søkvæsthuset (Royal
Danish Naval Museum** ex **Naval Hospital)**
1755, conversion 1989
Overgarden oven Vandet 58, Christianshavns
Kanal

[Islandsbrygge]

The hospital consisted of two parts: the simple
small two-storey palace on Overgarden oven
Vandet, and an L-shaped less architecturally
ambitious range to the south. In 1989 it was
converted into a naval museum which now contains nearly 300 ship models.

Classicism 1760–1798

33Ac **Sølvgades Kaserne (barracks)** now **Danske Statsbaner (Danish State Railways offices)** 1765–71

Sølvgade 40

Nicolas-Henri Jardin

Østerport

Every absolute monarchy needed an army which needed barracks. Apart from their size, these are remarkably free of the architectural rhetoric of militarism. The ends of the two four-storey 'F'-shaped (for 'Frederik'?) mansarded brick blocks face each other across a slightly acute corner where the modest entrance gate is set in a concave wall. To the street, the centre and end bays of each block are set forward slightly, and the corners of the projections are decorated with quoins. Jardin was a longer-lived contemporary of Eightved; his more famous work in Copenhagen is the contemporary Marble Church **34**.

34Ah **Marmorkirken ('Marble Church'** or **'Frederik's Church')** 1770, 1874–94

Frederiksgade

Nicolas-Henri Jardin, Ferdinand Meldahl

[none]

Work on the Marble Church which Eigtved had intended as counterpart to Frederiksstad 's central octagonal space was started with the rest of the building of the quarter. His first design of 1752 proposed a circular nave supporting a very tall drum surmounted by a slightly extended hemispherical dome topped by a tall lantern. There were to be towers to the north and south. After Eigtved's death in 1754 work continued to a modified design by Jardin but in 1770 the funds ran out and work stopped. The twin circular walls, the inner with alternating piers and arches giving on to a continuous ambulatory, had only reached the level of the springing of the drum. While in the

43

Classicism

following century many architects made pro-
posals for its completion, including one by C.
F. Harsdorff which would have converted it into
a very plausible replica of Rome's Pantheon,
and a chilling Neoclassical contribution from C.
F. Hansen, nothing was done and it remained
unfinished.

The unused hulk lay in this condition until 1874
when Carl Frederik Tietgen, an industrialist,
bought the it from the state and commissioned
Meldahl to complete it. He designed the col-
umned porch and the dome. This is 30 metres

(100 feet) in diameter and was modelled on
that of Michelangelo's larger dome at St Peter's, Rome. Its elegant silhouette and gilding
now supply one of Copenhagen's few land-
marks when seen from the sea. It can be
climbed in the mornings and provides a good
view of Frederiksstad. The church was finally
consecrated in 1894 when the flats which now
provide its setting were also built.

☞ Just to the north on Bredgade is the **Alexan-
der Newski Kirke** (Russian Orthodox Church) of
1881–83, designed by David Grimm.

35Ak   Harsdorffs Hus 1779–80

Kongens Nytorv 3–5

Caspar Frederik Harsdorff

▧ [Kongens Nytorv]

Harsdorff's most famous work is the burial chapel
for Frederik V at Roskilde Cathedral (*see* Excursions), but his more modest works in Copenhagen
where he was a professor at the Academy also
demonstrate his French-influenced classicism.
Here, the design of two houses on a site with an
obliquely angled corner provided an opportunity
for a small virtuoso display of contra-classical
ambiguity. It originally formed a small urban
composition with the earlier Royal Theatre to the
west. The left-hand house has five bays, the very
slightly projecting end one of which with its
segmental window hood is reflected across the
axis of the second house whose entrance is
round the corner in Tordenskoldgade. The pilas-

ters of the giant order of this second house have
their Ionic capitals the wrong way round and
buried in the wall: all we see are the ends of their
volutes. The delicate relief in the pediment is by
the sculptor Just Wiedewelt who often worked
with Harsdorff and who executed the tomb of
Frederik V at Roskilde (see Excursions).

**36Ah   Blå, Gul og Vestindisk Pakhuse (Blue,
Yellow and West Indies warehouses)**
1779–81 (Vestindisk), 1781–83 (Blå)

Toldbodgade

Caspar Frederik Harsdorff, G. E. Rosenberg

▧ Østerport

Harsdorff's practice was not limited to grand or
domestic work: here are two huge brick warehouses he designed, the Blue and Vestindisk, preserved examples of the utilitarian type found all
round the Baltic and which used to line Copenhagen's harbour front. Each follows one of the standard patterns: the gabled central bay and the ends
contain floor-to-ceiling doors for the receipt and
dispatch of goods and materials while the outer
bays have regular smaller windows. The Yellow
Warehouse, by Rosenborg, is of quite a different type:
a low block with many full-height windows. The Blue

Gul Pakhuse (Yellow warehouse)

Blå Pakhuse (Blue warehouse)

Vestindisk Pakhuse (West Indies warehouse)

and Yellow Warehouses were converted into flats in the 1970s. The Vestindisk building now houses the collection of plaster casts of the Danish Academy.

☞ Other examples of warehouses include that at Gammel Dok **65** and Eigtveds Pakhus **159**, both in Christianshavn.

37Ah **Medicinshistorisk Museum** ex **Kirurgisk Akademi (Historical Medical Museum** ex **Academy of Surgeons)** 1785–87

Bredgade 62
Peter Meyn

Østerport

Meyn's body of work was small, this is the largest building he designed in Copenhagen. A tall free-standing block with a mansard, the design of the elevation to Bredgade with its emphasis on the projecting and decorated end bays owes much to de Thurah. The accessible interior, however, houses at its centre an amphitheatre for surgical opera-tions whose shape and coffered half-dome with lantern are more characteristic of the Neoclassi-cism of the Enlightenment.

☞ The Kunstindustrimuseum **30**, the former Frederik's Hospital, is a little further north; on the opposite side of Bredgade is the former Opera House **20**.

38Ah **Screen, Amaliegade** 1794

Amalienborg Plads
Caspar Frederik Harsdorff

[Kongens Nytorv]

The royal palace, Christiansborg, was destroyed by fire in 1794, and the homeless royal family bought all four palaces of Amalienborg. Harsdorff was commis-sioned to rebuild the southerly two for the king and crown prince, and to connect them with this elegant timber screen. Its order is the Ionic which Harsdorff favoured for his secular work.

Classicism

39Ak **Gustmeyers Gård** 1796
Ved Stranden 14
Johan Martin Quist

This small palace was built for Consul Gustmeyer
by master builder Quist who, while relying on
Harsdorff's work for his models, was able to get
his Ionic capitals the right way round.

40Ak **Erichsens Palæ** 1797–99
Holmens Kanal 2–4/Kongens Nytorv
Caspar Frederik Harsdorff

[Kongens Nytorv]

Harsdorff's career spans late classicism and the
thoroughgoing Neoclassicism of, for example,
Hansen. This fine house named after its original
owner demonstrates the emergence of Greek
architecture as a source to be preferred to
Roman or Parisian; the correct Ionic temple front
raised on a plain base was the first in Copenhagen.
The reliefs in the pediment are by G. D. Gianelli.
The building is now occupied by a bank and the
splendid contemporary interiors by J.-J. Ramée
are inaccessible.

41Be **Bymuseum** and **Søren Kierkegaard
Samling (City Museum)** late 18th century
Vesterbrogade 59

The City Museum has been housed in this small
Neoclassical mansion since 1956. The collection includes interesting material illustrating the
history of Copenhagen, and the garden at the
front has been modelled to represent the city in
1500. The street to the east, Absalons Gade, has
been laid out with examples of the history of
Copenhagen's street furniture.

Garden model: 'Copenhagen in 1500'

Neoclassicism 1799–1847

42Be **Chinese Pavilion** 1799–1800, **Apis Temple**
1802–04
Frederiksberg Have
Andreas Kirkerup, Nicolai Abildgård

  Frederiksberg

The architects of Neoclassicism were eclectic,
finding inspiration not only in the classical forms
revealed by archaeology but in *any* strongly
flavoured exotic architecture. Sir William Chambers had introduced 'chinoiserie' to eighteenth-
century England, and Danish traders had connections with China. When the park at Frederiksberg
was remodelled in the English style, these two
pavilions were provided. The Apis Temple which
terminates the axis at the top of a small hill was
designed by Nicolai Abildgård (who built himself
the summer house **45** at Virum). The pediment of
the Corinthian portico contains a relief the bull
Apis. The striking red-painted and finely detailed
Chinese Pavilion which nestles in the greenery of
its island is by Kirkerup and is one of two in
Copenhagen; the other is at Tivoli **57**.

Chinese Pavilion

Apis Temple

43Bb **Sophienholm** 1800
Nybrovej, Lyngby
Joseph-Jacques Ramée

  Sorgenfri

Like his contemporary C. F. Hansen, Joseph-
Jacques Ramée's career started in Holstein where
he designed country villas for the merchants of
Hamburg and Altona. His subsequent career
included buildings in Denmark, here a villa and
park for an industrialist, and later work in the
United States. Like Hansen too, he was influenced
by French Romantic Classicism; unlike him, he
used almost no conventional classical ornament
with results such as the raw staccato composition for this house.

Neoclassicism

44Ag **Meyns Pavilloner (pavilions)** 1803–04
Kronprinsessegade
Peter Meyn

  Nørreport

Kronprinsessegade was laid out after the fire of 1795 and Meyn, better known as the architect of the Academy of Surgeons **37**, designed this row of little Neoclassical cubic pavilions and the railings between them as a boundary to Rosenborg Have. They were intended to house shops but were never a commercial success.

  ☞ Rosenborg **3** lies to the west of the park, Dronningensplads **125** to the west. The house at Kronprinsessegade 30–32 dates from 1806–07

and its interior was converted in 1990 to house the **Davids Samling**, a fine collection of Persian illuminated manuscripts. It was designed by Vilhelm Wohlerts Tegnestue, who twenty years earlier had designed the first stage of the Louisiana Art Gallery and Museum **138**.

45Bb **Summer house** 1805
Spurveskjul 4, Virum
Nicolai Abildgård

  Sorgenfri

Abildgård was both a painter and an architect. This small but important country summer house has a classical temple-like form and details. Its roof, however, is of romantic rustic thatch whose necessarily steep pitch produces the very pointed 'pediments' on the gable ends and over the centre. The fusion of the two sensibilities which the house suggested has pervaded much Danish domestic architecture ever since, and especially at the beginning of the twentieth century. It is now hemmed in by trees and almost invisible.

46Be **Søholm** 1805–09
Søholm Park, Gentofte
Christian Frederik Hansen

  Emdrup, Ryparken

Most of the villas Hansen designed earlier in his career were in Holstein and in and around Hamburg; this is the first of the few he later designed in Denmark. The hip-roofed two-storey block is raised on a basement and flanked by single-storey wings. The garden side has an attic loggia. In 1982–84 the building was converted for use as offices by David Bretton-Meyer.

47Aj **Domhuset, Arrestbygning (Town Hall, Courthouse and Prison)** 1805–15

Nytorv

Christian Frederik Hansen

Hansen's first career had been in Germany where he had first developed his Romantic Classical architectural language. The fire in Copenhagen of 1795 and the bombardment of 1807 gave him the opportunity for his second. His public debut in Copenhagen was the first building in what was intended to be the reconstruction and transformation of the centre of the city after these two disasters. Some of the materials for the new building came from Christiansborg Slot. The site for the large new Town Hall and Courts was south of one side of the city's oldest open spaces, Gammel Nytorv. The Town Hall is planned around four courtyards and the dignified giant Ionic portico gives access to a deep hall running between them. The sheer walls of the wings are carefully articulated by the minor entrances (the right-hand one provided access to the courts) and groups of three windows above. The inscription in the pediment 'MED LOV SKAL MAN LAND BYGGE' is from a thirteenth-century legal decree and means 'With the law man builds the land'. The building has not been used as the Town Hall since 1905 when the new Rådhus **71** to the west was finished.

This building is linked to the prison to the south by the twin bridges that span Slutterigade on arches. The façade of the prison is a splendid compendium of the Romantic Classical motifs of

incarceration: the rusticated base and door are contrasted with the flat rendering above in which are placed the aggressively hooded small windows of the cells. Note also the gate to the prison yard to the west on Hestemøllestræde.

Neoclassicism

48Bf Øregård Museum ex **manor house** 1806
Ørehøj Allé 2, Gentofte
Joseph-Jacques Ramée

   Bernstorfssvej

In his successor to Sophienholm **43** Ramée used
the same blocky undecorated composition of a
three-storey central block containing the important rooms flanked by lower wings, but the
proportions are less abrupt than those of the
earlier building.

☞ At the bottom of the hill at the back of the
house is the large white **Gentofte Hovedbibliotek**, the public library, of 1984–85 designed by Henning Larsens Tegnestue. To the
west at Adolphsvej 25 is the large **Kildeskovhall**

(sports hall and swimming pool) of 1966–72
designed by Karen and Ebbe Clemmensen. Each
of its three linked pools is housed in a separate
fully glazed pavilion with a delicate space-frame
roof structure.

49Aj Metropolitan School 1811–15
Fiolstræde 4–6
Christian Frederik Hansen

An Act of 1814 provided for universal education
and prompted a programme of new school building. This former school has two plain entrance
wings flanking on the first floor a large hall lit by
simple arched windows.

**50Aj Vor Frue Kirke (Our Lady's Church,
Copenhagen Cathedral)** 1811–29
Nørregade
Christian Frederik Hansen

There has been a church on this site since the
twelfth century, and it has always been Copenhagen's most important. The previous one was
severely damaged by fire in 1728 and again in the
bombardment of 1807. The church was last
restored in 1977–79 by Vilhelm Wohlert. Hansen
built within the walls of the previous structure, but
produced a radical new design: an axially arranged counterpart to his centralised Slotskirke
53. The nave is lined with unfluted Greek Doric
colonnades raised on arched bases set in from
the original outer walls to provide ambulatories.
The whole is roofed with a coffered barrel vault
whose form follows that of L.-E. Boullée's mega-
lomaniac project for the Bibliothèque Royale in
Paris and which terminates in the coffered half
dome to the apse. Light is provided both through
windows at the level of the colonnade and through

rooflights in the vault. The only non-architectural decoration is provided by Thorvaldsen's sculptures of the Twelve Apostles in the nave and of Christ in the altarpiece.

The treatment of the exterior offers a fine example of the Romantic Classical design method in which features or intense episodes of architectural activity are set against expanses of flat or geometrically primitive surfaces. The entrance is marked by the fluted Greek Doric portico, the first use of the Doric order in Copenhagen. Above this rises the fine square tower in two stages. (Plans of 1910 by Carl Brummer, and Carl Jacobsen's offer of money, to convert this stark arrangement to something more authentically 'Danish' by adding a spire fortunately came to nothing.) The semi-circular apse has a single door on the main axis of the church.

☞ Facing the entrance of the church across Bispetorvet is the **Bispegård**, the Bishop's Palace of 1732, restored in 1896 by Martin Nyrop; its courtyard is inaccessible. The University **54** and University Library **58** are to the north and Hansen's Metropolitan School **49** lies to the east.

1Aj Soldins Stiftelse (almshouse) 1812–15
Skindergade 34/Dyrkøb 1/Fiolstræde
Christian Frederik Hansen

The only clue that this simple four-storey block is by Hansen is provided by the severe porch to the carriage gate. The building is 'U'-shaped and has a small courtyard facing Dyrkøb.

☞ To the south, between Skindergade 34 and Vimmelskaftet, is **Jorcks Passage**, an 'arcade' without a roof, seedy, ungentrified, but used; the shop fronts are separated by a projecting composite order surmounted by cherubs. To the east, at Skindergade 5, is the small **Press Centre** of 1974 designed by Erik Korshagen of Juul Møller architects—its neat and considered curtain wall was one of the first in the old city.

Neoclassicism

52Bb**Hørsholm Kirke (church)** 1820–22

Hørsholm

Christian Frederik Hansen

🚉 Rungsted Kyst

This church was built when the castle of Hirscholm which stood on the site was demolished to provide materials for Hansen's reconstruction of Christiansborg Slot after the fire of 1794. It stands on its own in a beautiful large park, the former castle grounds. The composition has the limpid and elemental organisation characteristic of all Hansen's work. The long body of the church has a simple hipped roof and slightly projecting wings that house the stairs to the gallery. Attached to this at either end are the square tower and apse.

☞ In the centre of Hørsholm, and north of Rungstedvej, at Hove gaden 55, is the **Tromm** (cultural centre), of 1986–88, another of Knud

End gable (church under scaffolding 1997)

Munk's circular confections. To the south-east at Dianas Have 11–77 is the fine **Dianas Have housing** scheme of 1991–92 designed by Tegnestuen Vandkunsten. Seven terraces of houses are arranged across a slope so that their height varies from one to three storeys; the spaces between are beautifully landscaped.

53Ak**Christiansborg Slotskirke (church)** 1826

Christiansborg Slotsplads/Vindebrogade

Christian Frederik Hansen

The Christiansborg Slot burnt down in 1794 and was replaced to Hansen's designs. Another fire in 1884 destroyed all his work except this wing, the royal church, which was reopened in 1997 after restoration following yet another fire.

At Vor Frue Kirke **50** Hansen used an axial scheme determined by the shell of the earlier church. The

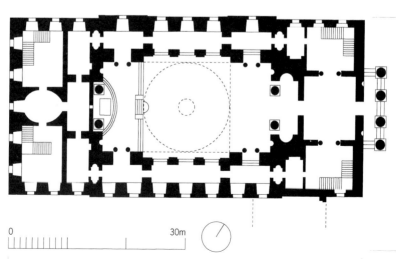

0   30m

spatial arrangement here is centralised: the most important feature is the large coffered dome with a small lantern. This stands on pendentives supported on coffered barrel vaults. The main axis running from entrance to altar is emphasised by screens that stand inward from the outer walls. Set in front of a small niche, the altar itself is almost insignificant, and its importance is further diminished by the pulpit placed in front of it in an arrangement similar to that at Hørsholm **52**. There is a box for the royal family above the entrance. The entablature of the Corinthian order provides a strong horizontal division: it separates the walls decorated in pale yellow *faux-marbre* and white columns and pilasters from the vaults and dome finished in beautiful matt white decorative plasterwork. Apart from that supplied by the lantern, the lighting is indirect and provided mainly by the two large Palladian 'thermal' windows in the barrel vaults.

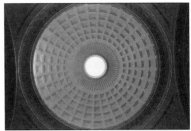

The exterior is composed of three elements: the dome rises above the box of the church and a simple Ionic portico set against a plain wall shelters the entrance. The side walls have slightly projecting centres which mark the tripartite subdivision of the near-square interior central space. The other carefully placed windows light the stairs and galleries.

☞ Thorvaldsens Museum **55** lies immediately to the west.

4Aj University 1831–36
Krystalgade
Peder Malling

An earlier building of 1731 was replaced by this monumental new university, one of the last schemes in the reconstruction of the city following the fire of 1794 and the bombardment of 1807. Although Malling was a pupil of Hansen, his design shows none of his master's sureness, and suggests the architectural turmoil that succeeded the certainties of Romantic Classicism. Its façade, in brick rather than the earlier stone or stucco, is composed of a series of staccato gabled bays separated rather than unified by flimsy pilasters. The interior contains examples of near-contemporary decoration including the entrance hall with (1844–53) frescoes by Constantin Hansen.

Neoclassicism

55Ak **Thorvaldsens Museum** 1839–48
Porthusgade 2
Michael Gottlieb Birkner Bindesbøll

The sculptor Bertel Thorvaldsen (1770–1844), having spent most of his working life in Rome, returned to Copenhagen in 1838. Before his death he offered much of his work and collection of antiquities to the Danish state on condition that it could be housed in a building to be financed both by himself and by public subscription. The king offered the site of the royal coach house immediately north of the Slot and Bindesbøll was appointed architect. Bindesbøll's design, a very late and probably the last important example of Neoclassicism in Europe, is noteworthy for its decorative scheme rather than its form. The museum galleries, built within the walls of the former building, are arranged round three sides of a courtyard which contains Thorvaldsen's grave. The fourth, west, side is occupied by the barrel-vaulted double-height entrance hall, whose exterior is marked by Herman Wilhelm Bissen's chariot-borne winged victory.

The decoration is extensive, lavish and startlingly colourful both inside and out. The flank walls of the exterior are covered in the 'frescoes' to the designs of Jørgen Sonne and carried out in coloured cement. Those on the north-east side show Thorvaldsen returning to Copenhagen and those on the south-west the unloading and transport of his sculpture. The brightly coloured interior provides a magnificent foil to the chaste white marble of Thorvaldsen's works: the walls are painted in fully saturated colours; the floors are in a variety of mosaic patterns; and the ceilings are painted in Pompeian style.

The basement was converted in 1968–73 by Jørgen Bo to house temporary exhibitions and a small permanent display about Thorvaldsen's sculpting techniques.

Eclecticism 1848–1914

6Bf

Lægeforeningens Boliger (Medical Association housing) 1853
Østerbrogade 57, 57a/Øster Allé 34
Michael Gottlieb Birkner Bindesbøll, Vilhelm Klein

Many of Europe's newly industrialised cities suffered from outbreaks of cholera caused by insanitary housing conditions and the lack of clean drinking water in the enclosed crowded blocks. The former were often countered by model housing schemes of which this is the earliest example in Copenhagen and the first to be developed on land outside the former ramparts. The original layout, subsequently doubled in size to the south, consisted of two parallel rows of very small, linked two-storey cottages facing each other across subdivided and private gardens. Communing conditions.

nal WCs were arranged in sheds at the back of the terraces. The simplicity of Bindesbøll's scheme, now finished in white and yellow brushed mortar, appropriately shows no evidence at all of his contemporary museum for Thorvaldsen, and its regular arched windows and simple slated roofs follow the tradition established in the housing at Nyboder **8**, and provided one of the influential models for subsequent efforts to improve hous-

»7An

Tivoli Gardens
1853 and many subsequent additions
Entrances from Vesterbrogade and H. C. Andersens Boulevard

Vesterport/Hovedbanegården

Copenhagen had pleasure gardens to the north at Dyrehavsbakken, but these were some distance from the city. When the demolition of the ramparts was started in the 1850s, the new Tivoli Gardens, established by private initiative and modelled on examples in London and Paris, were among first uses to be found a site on the vacant land. The present lake is a remnant of the moat, its form following that of one of the bastions. While the Gardens are now one of the city's main tourist attractions and are always crowded, they offer an extraordinary condensation of over a century's history of the forms of popular enter-

Chinese Theatre of 1874

Eclecticism

tainment. These now range from the simple pleasures of the classical pantomime in the tradition of the *commedia dell'arte* and set in Vilhelm Dahlerup's exuberant open air **Chinese Theatre** of 1874, to the more up-to-date small roller coaster in the south-east corner. Between these a variety of attractions is housed in pavilions whose decorative styles range from the pretentious to the kitsch, all disposed in a finely landscaped and well-maintained setting. The **Concert Hall**, built in 1956, was one of the few buildings aspiring to conventional architecture, but its decoration was contaminated by its frivolous setting. Its predecessor had become one of Copenhagen's few casualties of the Second World War and was blown up in 1944 by occupying German forces.

58Aj

University Library 1857–61
Fiolstræde 1/Frue Plads
Johan Daniel Herholdt

The earlier University Library housed in the roof of the Trinitatis Kirke **9** was destroyed by fire in 1728; this is its replacement on a site next to the new University **54** of 1831–36. A long fireproof shed with a cast-iron structure is enclosed in a shell of finely laid red Danish brick. Internally, two storeys of bookstacks are ranged on either side of a central barrel-vaulted 'nave'. The neat elevation to Fiolstræde has pairs of arched windows between piers which mark the alternate bays of the iron structure. The piers and arches, here blind, are continued on the gabled end facing Frue Plads and the single large window indicates the position of the internal vault. The architecture suggests that Herholdt was familiar with the German *Rundbogenstil*, but he derived the smaller features and patterned brickwork from the northern Italian examples which he had studied.

☞ Herholdt also designed the fine large **Grøns Pakhus** (warehouse) of 1860–62 in pink brick at Holmens Kanal 7. To the west of the north end of the Library at Krystalgade 25–27 is the former **Zoological Museum** of 1863–69. It was designed by Christian Hansen, architect of the Municipal Hospital **59**, and has at the centre of its rectangular plan a fine atrium in an Italianate version of the *Rundbogenstil*.

9Ab Municipal Hospital 1859–63

Øster Farimagsgade 5

Christian Hansen

Nørreport

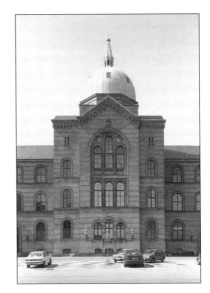

The earlier eighteenth-century hospital in Bredgade **30** had become increasingly inadequate, and the opportunity of a very large site made available by the dismantling of the ramparts led to the building of this new one. It was planned according to the modern principles of hospital design developed by Florence Nightingale among others in the aftermath of the Crimean War (1854–56). The wards are set at some distance apart to allow ample cross-ventilation and they are symmetrically disposed across the whole site, one side for men, the other for women.

Christian Hansen (1803–83) had worked in Athens with his brother Theophil (1813–91) and brought to the hospital his detailed knowledge of Byzantine architecture, here carried out in a yellow brick now weathered to a dull grey. Every opening is arched, and the surfaces are remarkably flat, the only relief being provided by the slight projections of the string courses and the angled and recessed bricks of the outer courses of the arches. Slightly more plasticity is provided at the central block of the front which has corbelled gables and a dome on an octagonal drum.

60Be Kongelige Veterinær og Landbohøjskole (Royal Veterinary and Agricultural College) 1860

Bülowsvej 13–17, Frederiksberg

Michael Gottlieb Birkner Bindesbøll

Bindesbøll's calm simple two-storey brick buildings for the College are arranged symmetrically. The style is routine *Rundbogen*.

☞ **Kristen Videnskabs Kirke (First Church of Christ Scientist)** is to the south, across Gammel Kongevej, at Nyvej 7. It was completed in 1967 and designed by Erik Christian Sørensen. The plan is a simple rectangle, its walls are in brick, and the very low roof is formed of shallow brick vaults of the sort used in church design by Sigurd Lewerentz.

Eclecticism

61Ab **Kartoffelrækkerne 1 (Workers' Building Society housing)** 1870

Øster Søgade and Øster Farimagsgade/ Webersgade and Voldmesitergade

Frederik Bøttger

Bindesbøll had provided simple rural terraces **56** for the first of Copenhagen's efforts at improved housing for the poor. These later terraces, nick-named 'Potato Rows', were developed by a work-ers' co-operative housing association. There are eleven small streets of tightly packed two-storey, three-bayed houses of pale yellow brick with red-brick string courses. The terraces are set very close together and enclose minute back yards. Architectural variation is provided in the gables: some are plain, others Italianate or Danish. The ensemble is now completely gentried, fully planted, and irresistibly charming. See also Bøttger's later housing at Østerbro **70**.

62Ak **Det Kongelige Teater (Royal Theatre)** 1872–74

Kongens Nytorv

Vilhelm Dahlerup and Ove Petersen

[Kongens Nytorv]

The tolerance of Danish authority to public enter-tainment has varied, but there have been four theatres on this site; the first was constructed in 1749. The present one was built when the prevail-ing models for public buildings were Parisian and Viennese (although the prolific and eclectic Dahlerup could also do Chinese theatres **57**, Byzantine churches **66** and elephants **64** if required). The plan is conventional: a horseshoe-shaped auditorium is reached via lobbies in the centre and stairs at the side. Externally, the composition is bi-axially sym-metrical: the elliptical dome which covers the audi-torium and fly-tower rises above an elaborately decorated rectangular block. The house is now used largely for performances of opera, but the inscription over the proscenium 'EI BLOT TIL LYST' ('Not only for entertainment') suggests an enlightened Lutheran view of education through theatrical performance.

☞ Substantial extensions to the theatre **161** were carried out in 1983–85.

63Ae **Housing** 1873–76
Søtorvet, Nørre Søgade, Øster Søgade
Vilhelm Petersen and Ferdinand Vilhelm Jensen

Not all the land released by the demolition of the ramparts was used for public buildings. Some was made available to developers like the architect Meldahl (designer of the completion of the Marble Church **34**). Here four blocks were treated as a single urban composition facing the Dronning Louises bridge. The models were fashionably Parisian both in style and in the large urban scale brought to Copenhagen for the first time.

64Bh **Carlsberg Brewery** 1880–83
Ny Carlsbergvej, Valby
Vilhelm Dahlerup

Enghave

The brewery originally established here by I. C. Jacobsen and his son Carl has outgrown its original plant and the buildings of various periods now occupy much of the surrounding area. The monumental buildings are confined to Ny Carlsbergvej and include Dahlerup's circular tower and gate with horseshoe-shaped arches of 1892, and the jokey water tower of 1901 which spans the street supported on four elephants in Bornholm granite and is topped with what may be minarets.

To the south of the Carlsberg site are two examples of Carlsberg's continuing architectural patronage, but these are only accessible from the brewery itself and can ordinarily only be glimpsed from Vesterfælledvej. They are the **Isotope laboratory** of 1965–66 by Paul Niepoort, and the **Bottling plant** of 1967–69 by Svenn Eske Kristensen, its curved brick façade facing a small park.

Eclecticism

65Al Pakhus, Gammel Dok (Warehouse, Old Dock) 1882
Gammel Dok, Strandgade
H. C. Scharling

[Islandsbryyge]

In 1984–86 this huge warehouse was tactfully converted to house the Danish Architecture Centre and the Danish Arts and Crafts Workshop. The architects for the conversion were Erik Møllers Tegnestue. It now houses offices, spaces for temporary exhibitions, a restaurant and a small but well-stocked architectural bookshop.

☞ **Eigtved's Pakhus** now incorporated into the Foreign Ministry **159** lies to the west. Other preserved warehouses include the Blue, Yellow and Vestindisk Warehouses **36** across the water.

66Bh Jesus Kirke (Church) 1884–91, tower 1894–95
Kirkevænget, Valby
Jens Vilhelm Dahlerup

Valby

This very lavish church, the burial place of the Jacobsen dynasty, was designed by Dahlerup while he was furnishing the Carlsberg Brewery **64** with eclectic ornaments. The nave is modelled on a Roman basilica, but it terminates untypically in a domed circular space containing the burial crypt. The free-standing campanile was added later.

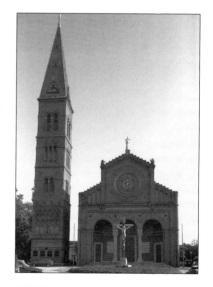

67Am Abel Cathrines Stiftelse (almshouses) now Municipal Offices 1885–86
Abel Cathrines Gade 13
Herman B. Storck

Hovedbanegården

While Dahlerup dominated Copenhagen's architectural scene with his delirious, large-scaled eclectic buildings, other voices had begun to propose a more modest programme, derived from local traditions, which in the Nordic countries was to become fully-fledged as 'National Romanticism'. This humble almshouse, built in pink-orange brick, has rooms arranged round three sides of a courtyard; a chapel occupies the fourth. The style, which in England would be characterised as 'Arts and Crafts' and perhaps ascribed to Norman Shaw, is unpretentious in the extreme.

8Ad Saint Alban's Church 1885–87

Churchill Park
Arthur W. Blomfield, design; Ludvig Fenger, execution

Østerport

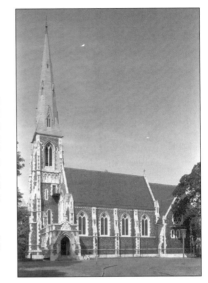

While the state religion of Denmark remained Lutheran, other denominations had been allowed religious freedom since the 1690s. St Alban's is a hard stereotypical church of the type built in suburbs all over England. It was funded entirely by subscription. It has a nave and chancel, and a single chapel to the north, all cleaned in 1985. While the appearance is English, most of the materials are Danish except the roof tiles which are from Shropshire.

☞ The Citadellet **11** lies to the north, Frederiksstaden **29** and Amalienborg are to the south.

59Ac Statens Museum for Kunst (National Museum of Art) 1889–96

Sølvgade 48–50
Jens Vilhelm Dahlerup and Georg E. V. Møller; extension 1995–97 C. F. Møllers Tegnestue

Nørreport/Østerport

The royal collections of art and antiquities had been kept in Christiansborg but after the fire of 1884 a new home for them was required. This new gallery, sited on land formerly occupied by ramparts, was built to house the paintings. Dahlerup and Møller's competition-winning design is unlovely and its siting banal: it faces the street junction with all the grace of a desk placed diagonally across the corner of an executive's office. There are no elephants or flourishes here: a central block houses the entrance under a triumphal arch of brick, stone, granite and travertine, and this is flanked by the two-storey blind and toplit galleries. These were originally disposed around two courtyards which have subsequently been filled in. In a misguided 'modernisation' in the 1960s the double-height entrance hall was stripped of its pomp when the former grand staircase was removed.

Included in the fine collection are works by the Danish painters Christen Købke (1810–48), who lived in and recorded life at the Citadellet **11**, and Christoffer Wilhelm Eckersberg (1783–1853) who, while better known for his meticulous views of Rome and Italy, also painted many of Copenhagen.

The gallery has always been short of space and in 1996 work started on constructing a competition-winning design by C. F. Møllers Tegnestue: an extension running the whole length of the present building to the north and facing the park.

☞ The Sølvgades Kaserne (barracks) **33** are on the corner opposite the entrance to the Museum. Rosenborg **3** lies to the south and the Nyboder housing **8** to the north-east.

Eclecticism

70Bf Kartoffelrækkerne 2 (Workers' Building Society housing) 1892–1903
Kildevældsgade, Østerbro
Frederik Bøttger

　Svanemøllen

Bøttger's earlier housing at Øster Søgade **61** was arranged in simple rows. Here, in a later scheme, the small quarter of about four hundred houses is symmetrically laid out in streets north and south of Kildevældsgade which is punctuated in the middle by a small square. The two-storey houses and their plots are again very small, and the gabled style and the materials tough: pale yellow brick with red-brick trim, and segmentally arched windows.

71An Rådhus (Town Hall) 1892–1905
Rådhuspladsen/Vesterbrogade etc.
Martin Nyrop

　Hovedbanegården

By the end of the nineteenth century, the old Town Hall **47** designed by Hansen had become too small to manage Copenhagen's affairs. A two-stage competition was held in 1889–90 for designs for a new one to be sited on land made available by the demolition of the ramparts. Martin Nyrop, a pupil of J. D. Herholdt, won with his design for a very large and tall block symmetrically arranged round two courtyards, one to the north covered with a glazed roof, the other more southerly one open. The council chamber, marriage room and archives are housed in the wing separating the two courts. At the time of its completion, the building was popularly recognised as a flagship of the National Romantic style which was emerging in the Nordic countries. Nyrop's choice of material, Danish brick, was itself polemic. Much of his detail was, however, eclectic and included borrowings from northern Italian and Dutch traditions: the vocabulary

provided by Danish architectural history was simply too poor to supply all that was needed for the ambitious Nationalist programme; and, though beautifully crafted, the building has nothing of the tectonic toughness of, say, H. P. Berlage's Amsterdam Beurs. The extensive decorative programme includes the statue of the Lur blowers by Anton Sofus Rosen, and the Dragon fountain by Joakim Skovgaard and Thorvald Bindesbøll.

The asymmetrically placed tower, the tallest construction in Copenhagen, can be climbed,

and to the left of the entrance there is a small bookshop and civic information about Copenhagen.

The square in front of the Town Hall was cleared of traffic and handsomely repaved in 1996 when the small but self-consciously fashionable transport information pavilion **183** was also constructed. (The new square would be further civilised by reducing the width of and calming the traffic on the absurdly wide H. C. Andersens Boulevard.)

2An Ny Carlsberg Glyptotek (Museum of Art and Antiquities) 1892–97, 1901–06
Dantes Plads 22, H. C. Andersens Boulevard/ Tietgensgade
Jens Vilhelm Dahlerup; Hack Kampmann

  Hovedbanegården

Carl Jacobsen gave his extensive art collection to the Danish state and to house it commissioned his favourite architect Dahlerup who designed the front half of the present building. Galleries are arranged round three sides of a square courtyard covered with a glazed dome. The façade to H. C. Andersens Boulevard is constructed of granite and brick and animated by an arched entrance flanked by wings decorated with linked triumphal arches, every surface enriched with carving.

Very soon after its completion, in 1901–06 the gallery was doubled in size when it was enlarged towards the back of the site with Kampmann's much more severely styled galleries arranged round two courtyards. The façade to Ved Glyptoteket literally and artistically turns its back

on Dahlerup's confections and hints at the arrival of Nordic classicism.

The most recent work to the gallery, completed in 1996, was the filling in of one of the courtyards of Kampmann's building. Henning Larsens Tegnestue's design provided for three floors of new galleries. These are reached by a stepped ramp which, climbing round their perimeter, finally gives access to the roof. The circulation spaces are finished in blinding white, while the galleries are painted in bright, saturated and characteristically Danish colours.

Eclecticism

73Ae **Søpavillionen** 1894
Gyldenløvesgade/Peblinge Sø
Jens Vilhelm Dahlerup

 Vesterport

Dahlerup died in 1907, but this is his last work in Copenhagen to be recorded here: a cheerful timber, minaretted club house for ice skaters, now used as a cabaret restaurant.

74Be **Åhusene housing** 1896–98
Åboulevard 12–18
Ulrik Plesner

While Nyrop launched National Romanticism with his monumental Town Hall, Plesner developed the style in his various designs for housing. These schemes, although all of them are quite tall and dense, are characterised by their general modesty and use of brick. They are frequently enlivened by corrugations to provide balconies, and by fun with gables.

☞ In the next block to the south at Åboulevard 8, the tiny **Bethlehemskirke** of 1935–37 is usually inaccessible. A very late National Romantic work in brick, its architect was Kaare Klint who completed Grundtvigskirken **95** and marketed his own range of pleated paper lampshades. See also other housing by Plesner at Danads Plads **86**.

75Af **Sankt Andreas Kirke** 1898–1901
Øster Farimagsgade
Martin Borch

Nørreport

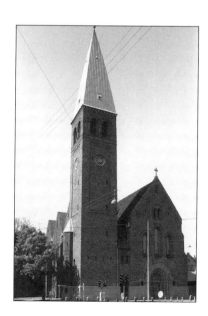

As Copenhagen continued to expand beyond its former ramparts, the new housing developments required churches and other public buildings. This one by Borch, one of the proponents of National Romanticism, is his masterpiece. Seen from the front, the composition consists of two parts: the nave to the right and the very tall, slender and plain tower to the right. The nave is very long and narrow, but the tower conceals a second, lower nave behind it. Further rooms for the parish are at the back. Although realised in brick, all the forms are derived from Danish Romanesque stone-built churches.

6Bf House 1904

Svanemøllevej 56, Ryvang

Carl Brummer

Hellerup

The district of Ryvang was one of the first sub-urbs to be laid out beyond and north of the nineteenth-century development of Østerbro, conveniently connected to central Copenhagen by both the railway and Strandvejen, the old road along the coast to Helsingør. Running north–south, the broad Svanemøllevej bisects the area and smaller streets run east–west. The area was developed with large, expensive villas, many of them now used by embassies and consulates. Brummer specialised in providing them, here a symmetrical composition with eclectic features placed in and against an almost completely flat façade of beautifully crafted brick. The large central window lights the double-height entrance hall and stair well. The gable above it may be of Dutch inspiration, but it is similar to that at the Abel Cathrines Stiftelse **67**.

☞ Another villa by Brummer is at Vestagervej 7, and other villas in the district include those by Rosen **78**.

7Am Hovedbanegården (Central Railway Station) 1904–11

Vesterbrogade

Heinrich Wenck

Hovedbanegården

The main passenger hall is roofed with twin timber-trussed arched roofs supported on brick walls which run, unconventionally, at right angles both to the line of the flow of passengers from ticket office to train and to the tracks below. At platform level similar timber trusses hold up the concourse but these are supported on lattice steel columns. The engineering structure is sur-rounded by a National Romantic decorated brick casing.

The consolidated blocks of shops which now fill much of the concourse were designed in 1978 by the railways' own architects together with Dissing + Weitling.

78Bf Houses 1906

Strandagervej 28 and Ryvangs Allé 6

Anton Sofus Rosen

Hellerup

The prolific Rosen designed each of these houses in the same year. The client for that on Strandagervej was the painter J. J. Willumsen, who got a bungalow (illustrated), cranked on plan and with one end housing his studio. The villa at Ryvangs Allé has a square plan sheltered by a pantiled roof of eight planes, and a half-timbered upper storey.

Strandagervej 28

Eclecticism

79Am   **Savoy Hotel** 1906

Vesterbrogade 34

Anton Sofus Rosen

Vesterport

Rosen's odyssey through architectural styles
and motifs continued here with an essay in the
Chicago style of the 1890s. The façade is an
early example of the almost completely glazed
wall. The structural steel frame of its three bays
are clad in elaborately worked bronze, occasionally gilded, and all capped with a frieze of
Sullivanesque ornament. The upper parts of the
façade were thoroughly restored in 1996.

80Be   **Elias Kirke** 1906–08

Vesterbros Torv

Martin Nyrop

Vesterport

Nyrop's National Romantic manner is here derived from genuine Danish examples rather than
the Italian of the Town Hall **71**. The façade is
constructed of stone, random rubble for the
walls, ashlar for the dressings to the arched
openings. The profiles of the twin towers are
slightly tapered. The interior is of brick; the nave
is separated from the aisles and galleries above
by arcades of segmental arches. The structure
of the timber roof is crowned by a continuous
rooflight of the sort more usually found in industrial or agricultural sheds. Like most Lutheran
churches, this one has a gallery at the 'west' end.

☞ To the north is the **Ny Teater** spanning the
continuation of Vodroffsvej, and to the west the
Bymuseum **41**.

Ak Christiansborg 1907–28
Christiansborg Slotsplads
Thorwald Jørgensen

Most of the royal residence designed by C. F. Hansen burnt down in 1884 and of his work only the Slotskirke **53** remained. The Stables and Marble Bridge **24** to the south-west were all that survived the earlier fire of 1794. The present building is an unlovely work by an otherwise insignificant architect. Its wavering Neo-Rococo façade to the square is clad in 750 different granites, one from each of Denmark's municipalities. The building has never been a royal residence and now houses the Danish parliament.

☞ The ruins of the first castle on the site, Absalon's castle **1**, are reached through the entrance of the main gate facing Christiansborg Slotsplads. The Slotskirke **53** is to the north–west, the Røde Kancellibygning (the 'Red Chancellery') **21** to the south-east.

2Aj Shops and offices 1907
Frederiksberggade 16/Kattesundet, Strøget
Anton Sofus Rosen

Here Rosen had one of two opportunities to design the major part of a city block, with shops below and offices above. While the building follows the palazzo format with a smudgy giant order supporting segmental arches and spanning the first and second floors, there is no central feature. Instead, the corners are emphasised with domed and pedimented pavilions. The columns of the order contain delicately detailed bay windows with fine *floreale* decoration in their spandrels, and to the extent that the building can be claimed as Denmark's only example of Art Nouveau, it has more in common with the Roman rather than the Belgian version of that style.

3Aj Palads Hotel 1907–10
Rådhuspladsen
Anton Sofus Rosen

Vesterport

Rosen here turned his hand to bricky National Romanticism, influenced perhaps by the site next to the Town Hall **71**. The symmetrical composition is dominated by the central tower whose only function is to show where the entrance is, but it does provide a foil to the Town Hall's. Much of the decoration of the exterior including the mosaic panels of 'Times of the Day' on the tower survives, but most of that of the interior has been destroyed.

Eclecticism

84Be **Bispebjerg Hospital** 1907–13
Bispebjerg Bakke 19–35, Bispebjerg
Martin Nyrop

Emdrup

The hospital was Nyrop's last large work. The
entrance and administrative wing are at the foot
of the sloping site, and beyond this the gener-
ously spaced wards are ranged up the hill with
garden terraces between them. At this point in
his career, Nyrop's style had become completely
purged of any sentimental residues of National
Romanticism: there are elemental blocks of brickwork, windows simply divided into squares; arches
sparingly used to denote entrances—very calm
and mature, and a little dull.

☞ Grundtvigskirken **95** is at the top of the hill to
the north-west.

85Aj **Housing and shops** 1908
Gammeltorv 8
Ulrik Plesner, Thorvald Bindesbøll

Plesner usually modelled his façades with sharp
corrugations of bay windows and balconies. This
façade, which can only be viewed frontally, is
organised quite differently. A nearly symmetrical
arrangement of four bays is disrupted by the full-
height shallow segmental bay windows which lie
under half the central gable.

86Be **Housing** 1908–09
Danas Plads, Danasvej 22–24
Ulrik Plesner, Aage Langeland-Mathiesen

Vesterport

The sites for Plesner's flats were usually conventional city blocks. Here he had the opportunity to
design one side of a small square. The six-storey
building has an L-shaped plan, and its ends are
marked with steep-roofed pavilions. The façades
are composed of Plesner's standard Nationalistic vocabulary of bays, balconies and gables.

7Bf Tuborg Headquarters now **offices** 1914–15
Strandvejen 54
Anton Sofus Rosen

Hellerup

Tuborg stopped brewing on this site in the early 1990s. Parts of the rest of the site were redeveloped (see **182**) and the former head- quarters building was converted for use as offices. This building takes the form of a large two-storey house planned round a large en- trance hall from which a grand staircase rises. The large roof has two sets of dormers. The composition of the front, which faces away from Strandvejen, is very slightly asymmetri- cal: the front door and the gable over it are off- centre.

8Be Haveboligforeningen (Housing for the Garden Home Association) 1914–20
Grøndalsvænge Allé/Godthåbsvej/Hulgårdsvej/ Hvidkildevej
Poul Holsøe and Jesper Tvede

Godthåbsvej, Fuglebakken

A 'National League for the Advancement of Better Building Practices' was established in Denmark in 1915, its aim to improve the stand- ards of rural self-build housing and that spon- sored by housing associations. This scheme for a model suburb was developed by the Garden Home Association. Serpentine roads provide access to plots containing either a single-storey cottage, a small two-storey house or semi-detached houses, all of an extreme modesty. For once, the model for the layout was not the Nyboder rows, but the picturesque theories of Camillo Sitte, and Parker and Unwin's Hampstead Garden Suburb in London. Unusu- ally for Denmark, however, the landscaping seems never to have matured, and the roads are not curved enough, suggesting that the models were insufficiently understood.

☞ Bakkehusene **94**

Hornbækhus 96: detail

Nordic classicism 1915–1928

9Bf **House** 1916

Gammel Vartov Vej 16, Ryvang

Povl Baumann

Svanemøllen

The flagship building of the revival of classicism in Denmark in the twentieth century was the Museum at Fåborg of 1912–15 by Carl Petersen. Completed a year later, this luxurious house marked the revival's first appearance in Copenhagen. While it is classically planned round a central courtyard or atrium, the symmetry of the entrance façade is broken by the artful placing of windows. The crude windows later inserted in the roof detract from the original plainness.

0An **Politigården (Police Headquarters)**
1918–24

Otto Mønsteds Gade/Polititorvet

Hack Kampmann, Christian Kampmann, Hans Jørgen Kampmann, Holger Jacobsen, Åge Rafn

Hovedbanegården

The short-lived classical revival which followed the exhaustion of National Romanticism in Copenhagen culminated in this extraordinarily large and chilling building. Even at an interval of eighty years, it remains unclear why an agency of a social democracy should need a building of the sort commissioned twenty years later elsewhere in Europe to represent the institutions of the fascist regimes. It is saved from bombast or kitsch only by being a very good example of its kind: scholarly and well built. The building, of a uniform four storeys, extends to the edges of its large triangular site, set back only at the entrance to the south-west. Single-banked offices lit

Nordic classicism

by regularly spaced windows are arranged round the edge of the site, while further accommodation within is reached and ventilated by lightwells and courtyards. Two of these are given special monumental treatment: to the south is a large circular court 45 metres (150 feet) in diameter. The ground floor is ringed by a colonnade of Roman Doric paired columns, and each floor level above by a matching cornice. The only significant precedents in Europe for this arrangement are to be found in the Villa Farnese at Caprarola and at Philip V's Granada. The roof of a square atrium to the north-east is supported by eight gigantic Corinthian columns which rise through three storeys.

The authorship of the building is complicated. Hack Kampmann made the original design in 1918, but he died in 1920 before the building was finished. Work was completed by his sons Christian and Hans Jørgen in collaboration with Holger Jacobsen and Åge Rafn. The latter's contribution is particularly significant as he designed little else apart from the small house at Ryvang **91**.

Politgården: circular courtyard

91Bf **House** 1919–20
Gammel Vartov Vej 22, Ryvang
Åge Rafn

  Svanemøllen

While involved with the design of the huge Police Headquarters, Rafn also designed this little classical house. Set parallel to the street, the long rectangle of the plan anticipates the house type identified in the jargon of the 1960s as 'wide-frontage single-aspect'. All the habitable rooms are spread along the south side facing away from the street. The nearly completely windowless street façade to the north is punctuated only by the stark porch, the single dormer window which lights the head of the staircase and the tiny circular window beneath. Its decoration is limited to the single plain string course.

92Be **Housing** 1919–20
Hans Tavsengade/Struenseegade, Nørrebro
Povl Baumann

The young Kay Fisker is usually identified as the inventor of the 'kilometre-style' of many of the developments in Copenhagen's inner suburbs sponsored by housing associations in the 1920s. But the older Baumann, designer of the yellow house at Ryvang **89**, was among the many other classically trained architects who evolved the simple housing format in which a five-storey strip was wrapped continuous round the edges of the site to enclose a large court. The similarity of all the buildings derives from their organisation: a repeating bay consists of a staircase giving access to flats on either side, and the architect's contribution was confined to how this regularity should be exhibited. Baumann's blocks on either side of the street are completely regular and the pattern of window frames (since replaced in plastic), set without surrounds in the plain brick-work, is carried across the staircases. Like those of the blocks in central Copenhagen built after the fire in 1795, the corners here are chamfered.

3Bf **Studiebyen (Model housing)** 1920–24

Rygårds Allé, Gentofte

various architects

Ⓢ Ryparken, Hellerup

The concern with housing design shown in the 1920s by the state and other agencies took many forms. This model estate was built to elicit designs for small low-cost houses from various distinguished architects. These are arranged on three streets and two closes. Rygårds Allé runs north–south; at the southern end of the site at its crossing with Lundeskovsvej are pairs of two-storey houses on either side, with four arranged in a composition around the corner. Further north, Rygårds Allé is lined on both sides with straight rows of very modest cottages (illustrated, by Peter Nielsen, August Rasmussen and V. Rørdam Jensen), the western side of which is interrupted by a classi-cally inspired arch to Sømarksvej. Most of the houses now appear quite unremarkable. The exception is the pair designed by Kay Fisker which terminate the close Lundekrogen. These combine an extraordinary simplicity and sophistica-tion and use the uniform tall openings characteristic of his work at this period. The central one on the first floor reworks the traditional gabled central dormer.

Cottages, Rygårds Allé

Houses, Lundekrogen

4Be **Bakkehusene (housing)** 1921–23, 1923–28

Bakkevej and Markvej, off Hvidkildevej, Bellahøj

Thorkild Henningsen and Ivar Bentsen

Ⓢ Fuglebakken

Like the Studiebyen at Rygårds Allé **93**, these row houses were commissioned by the Copenhagen Public Housing Association ('KAB') for poor fami-lies. The modest bungalows, their inhabitable attics lit by dormers, are laid out in continuous rows 180 metres (nearly 600 feet) long and some of the streets extend to the south beyond the open space, Rødkilde Plads. Every house has both a front and back garden. They are built of 'poor' mid-red and yellow bricks with pantiled roofs. Gentrified, and with well-tended gardens, the scheme now presents a benign image of dense suburban living.

Nordic classicism

95Be **Grundtvigskirken (Grundtvig memorial church)** 1921–40

Bjerget, Frederiksborgvej, Bispebjerg

Peter Vilhelm Jensen Klint, Kaare Klint

Emdrup

A competition was held in 1913 for a memorial to the Danish educational reformer N. F. S. Grundtvig (1783–1872). This was won by Peter Klint with his scheme for a church to be set in a square of housing. The design is a hugely enlarged version of the traditional Danish village church with a tower surmounted by a stepped gable and the same width as nave and aisles combined. Klint died in 1930 when only the tower of the church and the surrounding housing had been completed. He was succeeded by his son Kaare, and the church was finally finished in 1940.

The church has a nave and aisles, and galleries extending beyond the aisles and increasing in depth towards the centre. The interior is a bricklayer's masterpiece: the position of every beautifully laid cream brick looks as if it had been considered. Nothing is allowed to interrupt the smoothness of the surfaces and the only inflection is in the very small cantilever of the course at the springing of the vaults' cross ribs, a slightly Moorish detail. There is no clerestory, so the nave is quite dark, while an appropriately intimidating glare is provided by the five full-height windows in the apse. The building is a late fitting epitaph for National Romanticism, and its last great monument in Denmark.

The Bispebjerg Hospital **84** is down the hill to the south-east, and the extensive Bispeparken housing **123** runs away from the church to the south.

Elevation to Ågade; see also illustrations pages 17 and 70

6Be Hornbækhus housing 1922–23

Ågade/Skotterupgade/Borups Allé/
Hornbækgade 5

Kay Fisker

Frederiksberg

A few years earlier, at Hans Tavsengade **92**
Baumann had provided one of the first examples of the 'kilometre style'. It was Fisker who
showed here how the format could be made
into a work of art. The five-storey block occupies a near-rectangle 185 by 75 metres (610
by 250 feet). Units of nine bays, each planned
around a staircase, are arranged round the
edges of the site without regard to aspect or
orientation. Each unit has regularly placed
identical windows (which run across the stair
landings) set in simple rendered surrounds.
The only departure from this implacable scheme
is at the entrance doors whose tall openings
have to extend down to the ground to allow
access. The only residual explicitly classical
ornament is the cornice supporting the eaves.

The enclosed courtyard, reached through
arches on each of the short ends, was one of
the first in such schemes to be landscaped for
the exclusive use of the inhabitants. The plant-
ing is now fully mature and its area of nearly a
hectare (2 acres) now offers residents the
pleasures of their own medium-sized park.

97Bf Øregård Gymnasium (school) 1923–24

Gersonsvej 32, Gentofte, Hellerup

Edvard Thomsen and Gustav Bartholin Hagen

Hellerup

Classicism here provided one of the most
influential and long-lasting models for organising
a school. Within a square plan, classrooms on
two floors and lit by regular tall windows are
disposed round a central 'atrium', an 'aula' or
assembly hall. The arrangement suggests community and avoids the need for corridors. The
wonderfully austere central space has a ceiling of
a segmentally arched translucent laylight hung
from the underside of the trusses which span it.
On the exterior, classical aspirations are demonstrated by the tasteful frieze under the eaves.

☞ See also the 'School by the Sound' **117** and
Kathrinedalsskolen **106**.

98Bf   **Housing, Ved Classens Have** 1924

Classensgade 52–68

Carl Petersen, Povl Baumann, Ole Falkentorp, Peter Nielsen

Østerport

The toughness of earlier large housing schemes such as that at Hans Tavsengade **92**, and the Hornbækhus **96**, was not continued when considerations came to be given to the orientation and aspect of the dwellings. The block here does not extend round the full perimeter of the site but is cut back on the south side to allow sunlight into the courtyard and views out of it. The façades are also less severe than those of the earlier schemes: the bays containing the staircases project very slightly. These humanising impulses were severely compromised by the lack of access from the dwellings to the open space: this was and is a public park separated from the housing by a high wall and reached only from the south.

International modernism 1929–1960

9Ak Offices for *Berlingske Tidende* 1928–30
Pilestræde 34
Bent Helweg-Møller

 Nørreport

Berlingske Tidende is Denmark's oldest newspaper and claims to be the world's oldest. Its proprietors have been enthusiastic architectural patrons, with an earlier building to the south of this one, and the latest the small building **176** on the opposite corner. The building here, restored in 1990–91 by Knud Peter Harboe, is a modest exercise in the *moderne*.

00Bf Housing, Solgården 1929
Sankt Kjelds Gade 16–20/Vejrøgade
Henning Hansen

 Ryparken

The attempts to find a format for housing which hugged the perimeter of the site, while allowing the orientation of the flats to respond to the path of the sun and avoiding overshadowed internal corners, were eventually to lead to the rationally oriented free-standing slab. This layout is a compromise: the perimeter block is broken and set back at the southern corner to allow more sun in to the centre and to provide an entrance marked by the two hip-roofed pavilions. The doors to the staircases are reached from the garden side and the building presents its back to the surrounding streets.

International modernism

101Be **Housing** 1929
Vodroffsvej 2
Kay Fisker and C. F. Møller

⬚ Vesterport

This building was a watershed in Danish architecture. The first project was designed in a stripped classical style, but the second, built version marked Fisker's wholehearted and masterly incorporation of some of the forms of European modernism into his earlier classical sensibility. The plan is complicated: two wings, their storeys set half a level apart, lie along the two long sides of the triangular site. The wing facing the water returns at the north end. Blocks of stairs and other services and lightwells connect the two. Although the building is finished in red and yellow brick rather than white rendering, the continuous rows of regular windows and the long cantilevered balconies owe much to the generic style and ideology which emerged, for example, at the Weissenhof housing exhibition held in Stuttgart in 1927.

☞ The housing immediately to the north, **Søfronten**, of 1990 includes an adjoining block, which unfortunately was unable to match its earlier neighbour's storey heights, and three free-standing blocks. The scheme was designed by Arkitektgruppen I Aarhus.

102Am **Vesterport shops and offices** 1930–32
Vesterbrogade 8
Ole Falkentorp and Povl Baumann

⬚ Vesterport

This was the first large modern office building in central Copenhagen and the first with a steel frame. It is planned around three courtyards. When it was built there were few definitive modern models for commercial buildings, and the façade to Vesterbrogade is 'modernistic': classically organised round a prominent central feature. The curved side to Meldahlsgade is free of classical influence. The building is clad entirely in deeply profiled copper sections and sheets which have lasted extraordinarily well.

☞ Ole Falkentorp also designed the Hotel Astoria **109** immediately to the south.

103Bi **Flæsketorvet (Meat Market)** 1931–34
Kødbyen, Halmtorvet
Poul Holsøe (Municipal Architect) with Curt Bie and Tage Rue

⬚ Dybbølsbro

Copenhagen's Municipal Architect was among the first to adopt European modernism and apply it to public buildings. Modern architecture's aspirations to hygiene are here entirely appropriate. The Market is a complex of buildings planned around a courtyard, all constructed of reinforced concrete frames, finished in white rendering and lit through strips of windows. It was being restored in 1997.

4Bf Blidah Park housing 1932–34
Strandvejen 221/Phistersvej, Hellerup
Ivar Bentsen and other architects

  Bernstorffsvej

Even the sorts of reformed perimeter block for housing exemplified by the schemes at Ved Classens Have **98** and Solgården **100** were attacked by the proponents of European modern architecture, many of whom advocated the free-standing block as the answer to problems of overcrowding and the lack of air and sunlight. Rather than *enclosing* a park, the buildings should *stand in* one. This was the first scheme of public housing in Copenhagen to adopt these ideas. Some twenty-six three-storey blocks all lying north–south are laid out in staggered rows. They are reached from the existing surrounding roads and off Phistersvej from a new loop road running between them.

Within the strict layout some variety was achieved; different architects designed different groups of blocks but all are built of buff brick, have flat roofs and projecting balconies. The modesty of the buildings, the fine matured landscaping and absence of large numbers of parked cars now make this an apparently civilised place to live.

5Ak A. C. Bangs Hus, offices and shops
1932–34
Østergade 27
Bent Helweg-Møller

  [Kongens Nytorv]

Helweg-Møller cornered Copenhagen's market in *moderne* commercial buildings in the 1930s. While the frame is clearly visible, the spandrels are continuous. Both these and the recessed columns are covered in large sheets of faience.

☞ See also Helweg-Møller's Svane Apothecary **108** of 1934.

International modernism

106Be   Kathrinedalsskolen (school) 1934
Vanløse Allé 44
Kai Gottlob

Vanløse

The organisation of the plan of a school with classrooms arranged around a central hall, developed in for example Øregård **97**, persisted through several decades. There the hall was two storeys high; here it is a monumental three, and lit through an enormous south-facing 'industrial' rooflight. The classrooms are reached via galleries running round the perimeter of the hall. The building is placed at an awkward and unclassical angle to the boundaries of its site so that most of the large windows of its classrooms can be oriented exactly to the south.

☞ See also Gottlob's later similarly planned 'School by the Sound' **117**. To the south-east, at Lauritz Sørensens Vej and Finsensvej is the housing area **Solbjerg Have** of 1977–80 designed by Fællestegnestuen (Jørn Ole Sørensen, Viggo Møller-Jensen & Tyge Arnfred). The layout is similar to that of the later Sibeliuspark **164**, a south facing open 'U', but the buildings rise to greater height: up to seven storeys. The prefabricated concrete structure is clad in timber and corrugated fibre-cement sheeting. To the east again, between Jernbane and La Cours Vej, is the large Neo-Neoclassical and combined **Handelshøjskolen, Det Sproglige Fakultet (Copenhagen business school and housing)** of 1985–89 and 1989–91 designed by Henning Larsens Tegnestue. The housing is contained in two crescents to the north, the Business School in the long straight wing to the south.

107Bc   Housing, Bella Vista and Bellevue Theatre
1934, 1931–32, theatre 1936–37
Strandvejen 407–433, Klampenborg
Arne Jacobsen

, Klampenborg

Built in three stages, this ambitious scheme, the first by the young Jacobsen (in 1934 he was 32), introduced to Copenhagen the vision of modern living and its associated white surfaces and large uninterrupted windows which the Weissenhof housing exhibition at Stuttgart had brought to international attention in 1927. (Although the Meat Market **103** had been the first arrival of any sort.) The first stage, the two- and three-storey housing to the south, is arranged around a green in a broad 'U' facing the Sound. The flats are staggered in plan so that each gets a view of the water, and all have large cantilevered balconies.

The second stage, to the north, was a lower building originally a restaurant but later converted into more flats. North of this the final stage was the Bellevue Theatre, now a cinema, but designed with a retracting roof for summer theatrical performances.

☞ Immediately to the south is the later terrace and patio housing **140**, 1961, and south of this the linked houses **131** of 1950–55, both also by Jacobsen.

8Ak Offices and shops ex **Svane Apothecary**
1934
Østergade 18
Bent Helweg-Møller

[Kongens Nytorv]

This corner building is a suave *moderne* para-
phrase of a generic commercial building in Chicago. The scale of the bay of the structural frame
is doubled by recessing the face of alternate
columns so that these are flush with the spandrels.
The cladding of the frame is held in place with
closely spaced bosses and the animals on the
splayed corner supply further decoration. The
serious game of the elevations is, however,
undermined by the overhanging 'cornice' which
turns down at the ends and travels, very
untectonically, all the way to the ground.

9Am Hotel Astoria 1934–35
Banegårdspladsen 2–4
Ole Falkentorp

Hovedbanegården

The little hotel is on a cramped site between a
railway cutting and the street. Cantilevered above
the ground floor are two floors of bedrooms on
either side of a corridor, the ends of which are
connected to free-standing escape stairs in drums
sliced by helical windows.

10Ai Housing, Vestersøhus 1935–39
Vester Søgade
Kay Fisker and C. F. Møller

Vesterport

Fisker's experience in designing the definitive
classical housing block at the Hornbækhus **96**
was useful when he came to design this scheme
on an even more extensive site. A bay of seven
storeys and seven rooms wide on the front is
replicated from one end of the 315-metre (1,040-
foot) long site to the other. The brick façade is
articulated by the delicately detailed part-recessed
and part-cantilevered balconies to every other
room, whose arrangement contradicts the symmetry of the planning unit, and unified by the full-
width balconies to the top floor.

International modernism

111Be **Housing, Storgården** 1935

Tomsgårdsvej 78–110/Hovmestervej

Povl Baumann and Knud Hansen

Ⓢ Emdrup

A very long, 230-metre (760-foot) five-storey block extends the full length of the site, curving slightly at its northern end to follow the road. The planning of the flats around each staircase is asymmetrical, and the party walls staggered on plan, so that all living rooms, each equipped with a cantilevered balcony, face south-east. The north elevation is, by contrast, almost flat and its windows are set flush with the outer face of the very utilitarian brickwork.

112Bc **Houses** 1935, 1938

Sølystvej 5 and 7, 9–11 Klampenborg

Mogens Lassen

Ⓢ, ℝℰ Klampenborg

The site of these three houses slopes steeply down to a small pond and the houses are entered at first-floor level. Numbers 5 and 7 were built first, the former for the architect, and both are very close paraphrases of Le Corbusier and Jeanneret's Maison Cook in Paris of 1926, although without the original's asymmetry. The house at 9–11, which looks like three separate houses, is quite different and original: three two-storey pavilions, two on one side and one on the other side of a mature tree, face the garden and are linked by a curved corridor and entrance wing at the rear.

☞ The **Skovsgårdsskole** (school) of 1949–51 is about a kilometre to the west at Skovsgårdsvej 56, off the main road between Klampenborg and Lyngby. It was designed by Hans Erling Langkilde and Ib Martin Jensen.

3Aj   Stellings Hus (shop and offices) 1937
Gammeltorv 6
Arne Jacobsen

Owing little to European modernism but a lot to Sweden's Asplund, this is a fine mature example of a city infill building on a sensitive site on the corner of one of Copenhagen's oldest squares. The shop fronts were made of pale-green enamelled steel. The upper parts of the façade are clad in square sheets of light-grey faience whose module determines the size and position of the windows and which gracefully negotiate the curved corner.

4Ap   Knippelsbro (bridge) 1937
Kai Gottlob, consultant
[Islandsbrygge]

The first bridge here was built in 1620 by Christian IV to connect Copenhagen to the new township of Christianshavn. The present one is the fourth; its central portion lifts and the watch towers are handsomely clad in copper sheet.

5Ak   Offices now **Arbejdsministeriet** 1937
Holmens Kanal 20
Frits Schlegel

Bent Helweg-Møller had earlier provided *moderne* office buildings for central Copenhagen (**105, 108**). Schlegel produced this much more elegant and timeless version, a modern palazzo, its façades designed with a debt to Auguste Perret. The reinforced concrete frame (now painted) is filled with recessed panels finished in pale-grey marble fixed with exposed bosses and containing pairs of windows which are regularly spaced across the façade. The corners of the block are neatly filletted like the blocks with which much of Copenhagen was reconstructed after the fire of 1795.

International modernism

116 Be **Crematorium Chapel, Mariebjerg cemetery**
1937
Mariebjergvej, Lyngby
Frits Schlegel

 Gentofte

The chapel is a tall cubic volume constructed of a reinforced concrete frame of three bays in a-b-a rhythm. This is exposed and filled with solid or punctured square concrete blocks. The service buildings are in a single-storey wing to the east, and an elegant glass-roofed loggia provides a dignified setting-down point. Schlegel had earlier designed another chapel at **Søndermarkens Crematorium** at Roskildevej 59–61, near Frederiksberg Slot **18**.

117 Bi **Skolen ved Sundet ('School by the Sound')**
1937
Samøsvej 50, Amager
Kai Gottlob

The diagram of the 'aula' school which Gottlob had used at the earlier Kathinesdalsskolen **106** was here modified. To shelter the entrance courtyard two of the wings of classrooms are extended beyond the elliptical central hall so that their entrances are no longer directly off the hall. While the elevations provide a clear transcription of the organisation of the interior, they lack a clear tectonic scheme and in 1997 were sadly in need of repair.

☞ See also Gottlob's earlier similarly organised Kathrinedalsskolen **106** of 1934. The Svagebørnsskolen **118** is across the road.

118 Bi **Svagebørnsskolen/Friluftskole (School for Weak Children/Open Air School)** 1937
Sumatravej 1/Samøsvej, Amager
Kai Gottlob

The outstanding feature of this school and the one that led to its becoming celebrated in early histories of modern architecture such as Alfred Roth's, is the two-storey wing of classrooms. On the façade facing the garden, each room is articulated with angled projecting full-height windows suggesting and providing ample sunlight and air. Behind this, the rooms on the first floor are reached by an enclosed fully glazed ramp. Two further wings, one housing the hall, the other the entrance, enclose a small playground.

☞ The Skolen ved Sundet **117** is across the road.

9Ba Gladsaxe Rådhus (Town Hall) 1937, 1953, 1985–86

Rådhus Allé/Sørborg, Gladsaxe

Vilhelm Lauritzen

 Buddinge

In the 1930s and 1940s, many of Copenhagen's outlying former villages became the nuclei for housing developments and were equipped with new town halls (see Søllerød **124**, Lyngby **122**). Lauritzen's design, won in competition, provided an L-shaped wing of single-banked offices which partly defines an entrance courtyard. The corridors on the east and south sides are lit with strip windows, while the offices on the other sides have full-height classically shaped ones. In 1953 the wing to the west was added.

The first building contained only offices. In 1985–86 a new glazed entrance hall and cylindrical council chamber in brick were added to the east, and two further office wings were extended to the north and west. They were all designed by Knud Munk ApS.

 Buddinge Kirke (church) of 1967–70 is at Buddingevej 293 to the east. It was designed by Ib & Jørgen Rasmussen and Ole Meyer. In brick, tile and pine, its lavish accommodation is arranged between crosswalls suggesting perhaps a village.

10Be Grundtvigsskolen (school) 1937–38

Magistervej 4

Poul Holsøe, municipal architect, and F. C. Lund

The school lies at the lower, southern, end of a carefully constructed linear park on an axis from Grundtvigskirken **95** on the crown of the slope to the north. The central hall arrangement was not used and the plan is highly schematic: to the north is the hall with its large windows facing the park, and to the south a long wing of classrooms looks over the playground and playing fields.

11Be Radiohuset (Broadcasting House: Danish Radio Headquarters) 1937–41, 1939–45

Rosenørns Allé 22/Julius Thomsens Gade

Vilhelm Lauritzen

This ambitious and complex scheme was built over nearly twenty years and provides an example of the maturing of modern architecture. The two elegant office wings, staggered in plan on either side of the entrance, were finished first. Their finish of cream-glazed tiles has worn well, but the windows have been replaced with frames thicker than the originals. Note the bravely modern tower for aerials to the north at the corner of Worsaaesvej.

Later, a complex of performance spaces and studios was added. The largest of these is the concert hall of 1939–45, its three main functions

International modernism

of entrance hall, foyer and fan-shaped auditorium clearly displayed in three different volumes. Where not glazed these are covered in the same tiles as the offices. The shallow arched roof of the auditorium unconventionally runs front-to-back. The interiors are lavishly finished in a variety of Nordic materials.

Aerials tower

122B   Lyngby Rådhus (Town Hall) 1938–41
Lyngby Torv, Lyngby
Hans Erling Langkilde and Ib Martin Jensen

　Lyngby

The five-storey building successfully commands one end of a small triangular park (now filled with cars and desperately in need of gentrification and pedestrianisation). Both plan and style are maturely modern. The single curved form houses double-banked offices to the south, and to the

north the double height council chamber is indicated by the very tall windows. It is clad entirely in grey marble from Greenland (a Danish 'county').

123Be   Housing, Bispeparken 1940–42
Frederiksborgvej, Tagensvej, Tuborgvej
Ivar Bentsen and various architects

　Emdrup

Earlier large housing schemes such as Blidah Park **104** were laid out in modern doctrinaire fashion with free-standing rectangular blocks. This scheme of a similar size mixes street-hugging blocks to the west and south, with a composition of linked staggered blocks to the east. The latter are, unusually, laid out to provide an axis of open parkland stretching between the Grundtvigskirken **95** on the summit of the hill (the 'Bispebjerg') to the north and the Grundtvigsskolen **120** across Tuborgvej to the south. Bentsen and Kooperative Arkitekter provided the site plan, and the various buildings—all of cream brick, all with conservative orange-pantiled pitched roofs and differing largely in the treatment of their south- or west-facing balconies—were designed by different architects.

a

d

e

g

h

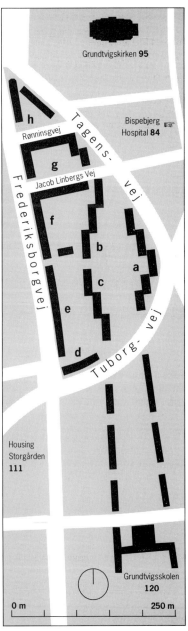

The eastmost range **(a)** of the staggered composition was designed by Frederik Wagner, and is
noteworthy for the attempt to incorporate dormer windows into the modern vocabulary. The
opposite sides **(b)** and **(c)** are by Edvard Heiberg
and Harald Petersen. To the south, facing
Tuborgvej, the slightly curved six-storey block
(d) which has shops on its ground floor was by
Knud Hansen. The enormously long, finely scaled
blocks **(e,f)** facing Frederiksborgvej, the southerly one following the slight curve of the road,
were designed by Vagn Kaastrup. The small
south-facing open court to the north **(g)** is by
Knud Thorball and Magnus Stephensen. The two
smaller blocks **(h)** to the north and at the junction
of Frederiksborgvej and Tagensvej are by Kaare
Klint and Valdemar Jørgensen. Although extremely
plain, they are the least influenced by modernism
and the design of their roofs and dormers owes
much to an earlier National Romanticism: Klint
was still working on completing Grundtvigkirken
across the road.

☞ Grundtvigkirken **95** lies to the north-east;
Bispebjerg Hospital **84** to the east. Grundtvigsskolen
120 and the Søndergårdspark housing are to the
south.

International modernism

124Bb Søllerød Rådhus (Town Hall) 1940–42, 1967

Øverødvej 2, Søllerød

Arne Jacobsen and Flemming Lassen

Holte

The plan consists of two rectangular blocks staggered on plan, and by half a level in section. (This popular format also appears in, for example, Fisker's Mødrehjælpen **135** and Munkegårds School **137**.) The block to the north houses the entrance hall on the corner, meeting rooms and on the first floor the double-height council chamber; the one to the south contains three floors of offices. The treatment of the exterior is calm and assured, beautifully inflected, and its contents made evident. The building is entirely clad in grey marble into which are inserted mostly square windows set flush to the outside. While the plan is academically modern, the materials and detailing of the interior and, for example, the diminutive copper-clad mansards which cap the exterior volumes all confirm that this is not a formulaic international modern building, but that a more local sensibility is at work.

☞ Holte became a favourite district for architects' own houses. Just to the east at Frederikslundsvej 22 is a **house** of 1970–71. Its design, by Max & Tulla Gudiksen, was heavily influenced by Le Corbusier's Maisons Jaoul of 1954–56. To the north, at Paradisvænget 24 is Knud Holscher's, in two severely planned rectangles.

125Ag Housing and shops 1942–54

Dronningens Tværgade/Adelgade

Kay Fisker and C. F. Møller with Eske Kristensen

In his work at the campus of Århus University, started in 1932, Fisker had shown no hesitation in putting a pitched roof on any otherwise modern form. This scheme brings the gable back to town in an ambitious scheme only realised over a long period. Gabled blocks of seven storeys line the east and west sides of the square, blocks with their eaves parallel to the street the north and south sides. One of Fisker's favourite motifs, the near-square window, is used to pattern most of the elevations (see particularly the backs of the buildings), but the recessed balconies have segmental arches. The blocks are finished in red brick with yellow-brick trim to the openings. The ensemble is extraordinary and the ingratiating folkloristic pattern-making not entirely satisfactory. It could also usefully be rid of the parked cars which now completely occupy the space.

6Be Houses 1943
Ellebækvej, Vangede
Arne Jacobsen

○ Vangede

This small suburban development is so modest as to be almost unnoticeable. Single-storey houses, square on plan, are set with their gables at a slight angle to the street and linked by screen walls. (In characteristic Danish fashion, it is not clear to which house the outdoor spaces so created 'belong'.) Only the very crisp detailing of the brick and pantiles and the careful, slightly mannered placing of the windows suggests the work of a soon-to-be internationally renowned architect.

☞ The modest brick **Stengård Kirke** (church) of 1962 designed by Rolf Graae and Vilhelm Wohlert is a little to the west at Gammelmosevej 250, Gladsaxe.

7Be Atelier houses 1943
Grønnemose Allé 21–49/Mose-skellet, Utterslev
Viggo Møller-Jensen

○ Emdrup

These very cheap houses were built for artists and craftspeople. Two terraces with courtyards for outdoor working run parallel to the lakeside while next to Grønnemose Allé a small row (illustrated) with balconies to the first floor overlooks a pond. The materials are startlingly inexpensive: walls of brushed mortar brickwork and roofs covered in corrugated asbestos cement sheets.

28Be Housing, Søndergårdsparken 1949–50
Gammelmosevej/Bagsværd Hovedgade, Gladsaxe
Poul Ernst Hoff, Bennet Windinge

○ Bagsværd, Stengården

The layout and style of this very fine scheme owe little to the patterns of housing proposed by international modern architects but a lot to what may be either Danish matter-of-factness, or the shortage of building materials in Denmark after 1940.

Some 200 small dwellings are laid out at a very low density round a large and now fully mature park (densely planted at its edges) runs north–south the length of the site. These are served by narrow roads which meander round three edges of the site to serve short streets and cul-de-sacs. None of theses streets are parallel, and those on the west side are laid out in a fan formation. There are very few private gardens and, for those

houses fortunate to face it, the open space extends uninterrupted up to their living-room windows.

Most of the houses are bungalows, but there are a few two-storey terraces to the north near the school and small shopping centre. The modest materials are yellow brick and pale-orange pantiles, and the larger windows are set in splayed rendered reveals.

International modernism

129Be **Voldparken housing** 1949–51

Arildsgård, Kobbelvænget, Husum

*F. C. Lund, municipal architect, Kay Fisker,
Edvard Heilberg, Viggo S. Jørgensen and K.
Larsen*

Husum

The scheme of 1,400 dwellings in free-standing
blocks is laid out in two parts. To the north a row
of five seven-storey slabs are oriented north–
south and set well apart from each other. To the
south lies a more complex arrangement of three-
and seven-storey blocks, some free-standing,
others joined at their corners to form L-shapes.
All the buildings lie in now matured landscaped
parkland. The buildings have a grand scale: solid
balcony fronts faced in scalloped asbestos cement tiles span between the widely spaced party
walls of yellow brick. Every block, of whatever
height, is capped with a hipped roof also clad in
scalloped tiles.

☞ The Voldparken school **132** of 1952 and 1956
lies on the eastern edge of the site. To the north
at Mørkhøj Park Allé 3–5 is the very large
**Blaagaard Statsseminarium og Enghavegård
Skole (State teacher training college and
practice school)** of 1962–66. It was designed
by Jørgen Bo, Karen & Ebbe Clemmensen and is
a fine example of the architecture and planning of
the 1960s and an alternative to the prevailing
brutalism with its palette of elegant materials
more usually found in contemporary corporate
buildings in North America: brick, copper and
glass. The large **Hoffmandsminde & Sankt
Antoni Kirke (nursing home and church)** of
1972–73 designed by Vilhelm Wohlert is at
Frederikssundsvej 225, to the west. The various
brick buildings are arranged in a long strip with
the church at one end.

130Be **Housing, Bellahøj** 1949–56

Bellahøjvej, Brønshøj

*Tage Nielsen and Mogens Irming and various
architects*

The site which lies along the brow of a hill was a
former country estate. A competition for its
development was held in 1944 and the winning
scheme proposed two groups of towers to the
north and south of the centre of the estate which
was to be developed as a park. The towers at
eight and ten storeys are of modest height but tall
enough to give each flat a view of the Sound. The
towers are not simple slab shapes: in plan their
two halves are staggered around the central
staircase and lift, and the floors of each part are
staggered again by half a level. Their façades,
although technically innovative and restored in
1996, are just a little dull. But where are the cars?

☞ The Bakkehusene houses **94** of 1921–23 are
down the hill to the east.

1Bc **Houses** 1950–55
Strandvejen 413, Klampenborg
Arne Jacobsen

☺, ☐☐ Klampenborg

The theme of 'linked' houses used by Jacobsen at Ellebækvej **126** was here developed on a small site south of his earlier Bella Vista scheme **107** to which this layout is similar: a broad 'U' facing the Sound. Here, however, individual houses of two storeys are linked by single-storey entrances. The square windows in the flank walls are to the first-floor living rooms and provide a view of the Sound. The roofs are stepped, and a shallow pitch is set against a steeper one: this might have been an innovation but it subsequently became a cliché.

☞ The later terrace and patio houses **140** are immediately to the north.

2Be **Voldparkens Skolen (schools)** 1952, 1956
Husum
Kay Fisker

☐ Husum

There are two schools here. The earlier, primary school, is housed in the collection of single-storey buildings to the east. The later is the secondary school of three storeys. Here Fisker used one of his characteristic plans (see also the Mødrehjælpen flats **135**). Two long blocks of single-banked classrooms slide past each other. Each façade of these blocks is treated very differently: the outer faces are almost entirely composed of the classroom windows, while the inner faces have staggered square windows to the corridors set in a field of brick. Where the blocks overlap, the gap between them is roofed to house a porch, a three-storey-high entrance hall and the main staircase which provides access to the whole building. The hall is beyond this. The same utilitarian materials employed for the nearby Voldparken housing are used in the school: yellow brick, and fibre-cement tiles for the spandrels to the classrooms and for the pitched roofs.

☞ The school lies on the eastern edge of the site of the Voldparken housing **129** of 1949–51.

International modernism

133Bh Offices for F. L. Smidth 1952–57
Vigerslev Allé 77, Valby
Palle Suenson

Valby

This assured, beautiful building was commissioned by a large engineering firm. Three wings of different heights are butted together, two of eight and two storeys in a line at right angles to the road and a third of four storeys at right angles to these. Their façades are formed either of very deep full-height piers of dark-red brick between which are the windows, or of full-height panels of the same brick. The penthouse of the wing nearest the entrance to the site has, like the eaves of the building proper, a most elegantly detailed oversailing roof edged in copper. Eliel Saarinen used large panels of brickwork at the General Motors Technical Center, Warren, Michigan, of 1948–56, but there the resemblance stops.

☞ To the south, at Carl Jacobsens Vej 25, several large factories and old office buildings constructed in 1913 which might otherwise have been destroyed were instead renovated in 1991 as offices. The architects for the renovation and the new linking buildings were Kristian Isagers Tegnestue A/S & B. Hjembæk Prætegård.

134Ai Offices for A. Jespersen and Søn 1953
Nyropsgade 18
Arne Jacobsen

Vesterport

Jacobsen showed here for the first time an awareness of models from North America. The solid tower to the north contains services; to the south the offices are supported on a daring structure of just four piers which support beams running the length of the building. Floor slabs cantilever outwards from these to the exterior which is clad in one of the first curtain walls in Copenhagen. This kind of architecture (and see the SAS Hotel **139**) requires precision in building, which it did get; and long-lasting materials and good maintenance which it didn't. At best, it now looks inoffensive.

135Bf Flats 'Mødrehjælpen' 1954–61
Strandboulevarden 127/Svendborggade
Kay Fisker

Nordhavn

These flats for single mothers are laid out in two seven-storey wings. These meet end to end but stagger in plan by the depth of a room. Communal rooms and the entrance are placed where they join. Each wing is simply organised with rooms on either side of a corridor. This just stops at the ends of the block, and each stack of rooms is given its own pitched roof and gable on either side of the corridor. The façades to the rooms themselves are regularly patterned by Fisker's favourite near-square windows set flush with the yellow brickwork. The building was later extended to the south with a third wing, again staggered and in matching style.

6Be Rødovre Rådhus (Town Hall) 1955
Rødovre Parkvej, Rødovre
Arne Jacobsen

Rødovre

Forming the west side of a later pedestrian square, the building is of extreme simplicity: offices are contained in a long three-storey slab. Its long sides are extensively glazed while its ends are clad in marble. The council chamber, also mostly glazed and perhaps indicating the openness of local government, projects from this behind the entrance.

☞ The Library **150** to the east, constructed in 1965, is also by Jacobsen. To the north, the cultural centre 'The Fan' of 1988 is by Dissing + Weitling **169**.

7Be Munkegårds Skolen (school) 1956–57
Vangedevej 178, Munkegårds, Gentofte
Arne Jacobsen

Vangede

There had been earlier Danish schools in which the classrooms were laid out in rows connected by covered ways. It took Jacobsen to make a masterpiece of the format. The large school is entered from a courtyard at the southern edge of the site. To the west are gymnasiums. Five covered ways extend north from the courtyard, three serving blocks of single-storey classrooms and two giving access to the hall and dining room. The covered ways end at a two-storey wing of special classrooms such as those for crafts. Each classroom looks south through full-height windows over its own little courtyard, and further light is provided by a clerestory in the split-

pitched roof. The plan has a severely diagrammatic quality which would alarm most clients and many architects, but the building itself combines rigour and charm. It was restored in the 1990s and the patios are now as lushly planted as only Danish and Californian patios can be.

☞ To the south-east, at Søborg Torv on Søborg Hovedgade, is a housing scheme **Høje Søborg** of 1949–51 by Poul Ernst Hoff and Bennet Windinge. The L-shaped six-storey building now looks utterly unremarkable, but its programme was pioneering: as well as the flats, the scheme contained other facilities such as a meeting room, restaurant and shop for the use of residents. To the north-east, the **Vangede Kirke (church)** of 1974 at Vangedevej 50, was designed by Johan Otto von Spreckelsen. As in this architect's church at Stavnsholt **156**, the influence of Louis Kahn is again evident.

International modernism

138 Bc **Louisiana Art Gallery and Museum** 1958, 1991

Gammel Strandvej 13, Humlebæk

Jørgen Bo and Vilhelm Wohlert

Humlebæk

Knud W. Jensen married three women called Louise. The art museum he developed from the original modest family house is named after them. The first phase is that to the north: a loosely arranged string of covered ways and exhibition spaces of various heights and at different levels runs away from the house and terminates at a restaurant on a small cliff overlooking the Sound. The buildings are simply constructed of white-painted brick with timber roofs and windows, and the covered ways have full-height glazing. The accommodation includes rooms suitable for concerts, recitals and readings. The ensemble is unmatched, the promenade which alternates views out over the gardens with the works in the galleries a delight, and the theatrically contrived arrival at the restaurant terrace (enlarged in 1991) with its view breathtaking. The art is worth a look, too.

More galleries were added in 1982 to make a second string to the south, and the circulation was finally joined into a ring by the entirely subterranean space, intended for delicate works on paper but now used for temporary exhibitions, constructed in 1991. The style of the later phases is not as forthright as that of the earlier, and in a garden the circular features and rooflights are distracting.

The gardens are used for the display of sculpture and outdoor installations: never has a work by Henry Moore looked so convincing as in this setting, and see Richard Serra's steel sheets set in the ravine below the restaurant.

139 Am **SAS Radisson Hotel** ex **SAS Royal Hotel** 1960

Vesterbrogade/Hammerichsgade

Arne Jacobsen

Vesterport

In the late 1950s, Jacobsen's commissions expanded in number and type, and most notably in this design for this hotel and headquarters for the SAS airline, Jacobsen abandoned 'Nordic' conventional urban forms and local materials for specifically transatlantic ones, especially those of the work of Skidmore, Owings and Merrill. The model here, copied all over Europe, is that firm's Lever House in New York of 1952: a tower stands on a slab, or 'podium', which more or less fills the edges of the site. The podium at Lever House, however, was raised above the ground on columns so that much of the site was available to pedestrians; here it fills the whole block. The tower contains eighteen floors of hotel bedrooms, and it remains Copenhagen's tallest building after the Town Hall. The less than substantial

materials of its façades do not stand up to such exposure or to weather or time.

The building was when opened an example of 'total design', and Jacobsen was commissioned to design many of the interiors, fittings and much of the furniture, but subsequent refits have destroyed the earlier integrity.

Bc Housing Ved Bellevue Bugt 1961

Strandvejen 447, Klampenborg

Arne Jacobsen

S, RE Klampenborg

Thirty years after the first housing at Bellevue **107**, Jacobsen designed this scheme next to it and north of the linked houses **131**. There are two parts: a three-storey block of flats lies at the back of the site; in front of this is a block of five single-storey houses lavishly planned around courtyards. The scheme is a *mélange* of transatlantic and Scandinavian ideas: earlier in the century the patio house had been developed by Mies van der Rohe and Hilberseimer, and in Denmark Jørn Utzon's houses at Kingo of 1958–61 were to become highly influential.

d Toms Fabriker (chocolate factory) 1961, 1971

Ringvej B4, Ballerup Byvej, Ballerup

Arne Jacobsen; Dissing + Weitling

S Ballerup

The factory for making chocolate products is contained in a large single-storey shed with a steel frame set out on a square structural bay.

The design format is 'a slab with things on the roof' (as spectacularly used by Le Corbusier). The slab is elegantly designed, and clad in uniform panels made up of small white ceramic tiles. Various unavoidable protrusions, flues, extracts, plant, are carefully clad and disposed on the roof.

The neat three-storey office building to the east was built in 1971 and designed by Dissing + Weitling.

Bagsværd Kirke 153

Social democratic pluralism 1961–1998

2Bb **Plejehospitalet I Ringbo (nursing home)**
1961–63

Granvej 14, Bagsværd

*Stadsarkitektens Direktorat (Municipal
Architect's Department, Hans Christian Hansen)*

    Bagsværd

The various departments of this home for the
elderly are disposed in a very large circle around
a park, although since the park's landscape has
become so dense, it is now impossible to perceive this or to glimpse any more than the
occasional spike of a very pointed rooflight rising
above the mainly single-storey buildings. Hansen
was a long-standing employee of the Municipal
Architect's Department, and his formal language
was very particular, and different for each job.

☞ And see the Bremerholm **143** and Svanemøllen
149 switching stations also designed by Hansen.

43Ak **Koblingstation (transformer station)** 1963

Bremerholm 6

*Stadsarkitektens Direktorat (Municipal
Architect's Department, Hans Christian Hansen)*

    [Kongens Nytorv]

These installations are usually hidden away and
are rarely given the dignity of a façade more
suitable for a superior car park or a department
store. If they must be visible, then Hansen's
elegant bronze grating covering a concrete box
and capped with a cornice/sun screen is a good
way to treat them.

Social democratic pluralism

144Be Nyager Skole (primary school) 1963
Nyager Vænge 14, Rødovre
Arne Jacobsen

Jacobsen's earlier Munkegårds School of 1957 had shown how groups of classrooms served by corridors and linked by covered ways (the 'comb' plan) could be successfully combined into an organic composition. The plan here is a

disappointment, neither as taut nor as successful. The various blocks are disposed so that it is possible to get from one to another, but there is no evident hierarchy of circulation. While the scheme is united by the continuous yellow brick walls, matters are not helped by the aggressive industrial profiles of the roofs to the gymnasiums (illustrated).

145Bg Housing district Albertslund Syd 1963–68
Albertslundvej
Fællestegnestuen (Viggo Møller-Jensen, Tyge Arnfred, Mogens J. Pedersen & Jørn Ole Sørensen)

Albertslund

This was one of two gigantic and contrasting housing schemes started at about the same time; the other was at Høje Gladsaxe **146**. About 2,000 dwellings are accommodated in single-storey patio houses, two-storey terraces and three-storey square blocks. While the intention was to provide a layout as comprehensible as an 'ordinary' town, the realisation is patchy, and the circulation and means of access to the dwellings is difficult and often far from ordinary.

The layout is strictly orthogonal. Some distance south of the railway line, a row of three-storey

blocks lines the new canal. A main road runs north of these, and smaller roads lead off this north and south to groups of single-storey 'patio' dwellings. A commercial centre is placed to the north-east on the other side of Albertslundvej.

The more dense parts of the scheme are now the most successful, especially those bordering the well-landscaped canal, although even here the amount of circulation and public open space seems confusing and excessive. The informally arranged groups of patio houses have, even after 'restoration' of the prefabricated building system, the air of squatter camps, and the usual flair with landscaping is missing.

☞ The church in the north-east quadrant of the layout at Gymnasievej 2 is the **Opstandelseskirken (Church of the Resurrection)**, of 1984, designed by Inge and Johannes Exner.

Canalside blocks

Patio houses

Be **Housing, Høje Gladsaxe** 1963–68

Gladsaxevej, Søborg

Povl Ernst Hoff & Bennet Windinge, Jørgen Juul Møller, Kai Agertoft & Alex Poulsen

The inclusion of this scheme in all the standard histories of modern architecture was meant to demonstrate how ruthless Stalinist methods of layout and building could successfully be applied to housing in social democracies. The state of the scheme some thirty years after its completion, and following a major 'restoration' and remodelling in 1990–92 of its failing industrialised building systems, suggests that those histories were almost right. On a greenfield site with not much else around, the scheme houses about 2,000 dwellings in five sixteen-storey slabs placed in a line on a ridge

and in a loosely strung line of nine-storey slabs to the west. There is a small shopping centre and a school to the east. A broad continuous landscaped promenade runs in front of the taller slabs.

In the restoration, the social and technical problems which the scheme had developed were tackled in a number of ways. The tall slabs were joined up at their bases to reduce the permeability of the circulation, and many of the outdoor spaces relandscaped. The failing pre-cast concrete cladding of the south-facing façades was removed and replaced by a smart new blue and silver curtain wall set forward of the original face to provide full-width glazed balconies for the flats. On a sunny day, the slabs with their populated balconies now present incompatible images both of a dense Mediterranean holiday resort and of a utopian socialist dream.

7Be **Præstebro Kirke (church)** 1965–69

Tornerosevej, Herlev

Inger & Johannes Exner

Herlev

The small church stands on a large site near a major road intersection. The square body of the church proper rises out of a single-storey podium housing confirmation, committee and service rooms, some of which look out over a walled garden. The church is entered and organised on the diagonal of its plan and is lit by a lantern whose light is filtered through baffles which descend over the altar. The materials are modest: brick inside and out, and timber. The enigmatic free-standing object whose brickwork appears to

be peeling away at the top is the bell tower; it signals the church's presence to the passing traffic.

☞ Other churches by the Exners include Islev Kirke of 1967–70 at Hvidsværmervej, Rødovre.

Social democratic pluralism

148Ak Danmarks Nationalbank (National Bank of Denmark) 1965–78

Havnegade 5/Niels Juels Gade

Arne Jacobsen, Dissing + Weitling

[Kongens Nytorv]

Jacobsen won the competition for this scheme in 1961. Work started in 1965, but he died in 1971 and the job was finished by his successors Dissing + Weitling. The only concession made to the important and sensitive location is to the trapezoidal shape of the site, otherwise this building provides another example of the transat-lantic 'slab on a podium' format. The podium here contains the banknote printing works and the five-storey slab offices. The slab has a thick plan punctured by three spaces: two open lightwells one of which provides roof light to the banking hall, and a closed one, the five-storey high entrance hall which contains a delicately detailed free-standing staircase. The materials are Nordic: marble for the walls of the podium and granite for the office façades. While the east elevation to Niels Juels Gade at least continues the street frontage from the north, at street level the pedestrian is given nothing to look at except marble, which palls after the first few metres.

149Bf Koblingstation (transformer station) 1966–68

Nyborggade 13

Stadsarkitektens Direktorat (Municipal Architect's Department, Hans Christian Hansen)

Svanemøllen

In the earlier station at Bremerholm **143** Hansen had exercised quiet good taste in a smart street frontage. He had no such inhibitions here. The various technical functions are accommodated in a series of linked boxes constructed of blast-proof concrete walls. Their timber shuttering has been left in place and capped with little playful mansards, the result suggesting a large Alpine MacDonalds.

3e Hovedbibliotek, Rødovre (public library)
1969
Rødovre Parkvej 140, Rødovre
Arne Jacobsen

Rødovre

When locating this library, facing the earlier Town Hall **136** which he had designed in 1955, Jacobsen had the rare opportunity to create a small pedestrian square. The model is taken from the work of Mies van der Rohe and Eliel Saarinen. The lining-up of the front door of the library with that of the Town Hall is the only geometric link between the two buildings, otherwise their disposition seems casual.

The library is contained within a single-storey windowless shed entirely clad in brown marble that matches that of the end walls of the Town Hall. Its plan was originally divided into three differently sized zones, but the clarity of this layout has been compromised by later alterations. The entrance provides access to a large

library on the right (south), and a smaller one on the left (north). Between them, a small combined exhibition and lecture space with a raised oversailing roof and clerestory lies beyond the reception desk. The very deep plan is illuminated by five courtyards. The materials and detailing appear coarse when compared with some earlier buildings by this architect.

☞ The Rådhus (Town Hall) **136** of 1955 is opposite. To the north, the cultural centre 'Viften' **169** of 1988 is by Dissing + Weitling.

3a Housing Farum Midtpunkt 1970–74

Birkhøjterrasserne, Nygårdterrasserne, Pantholmterrasserne, Frederiksborgvej, Farum

Fællestegnestuen (Jørn Ole Sørensen, Viggo Møller-Jensen, Tyge Arnfred)

Holte

About 1,500 dwellings are consolidated into a single design which occupies the whole site. The entire surface of the ground is devoted to moving or parked cars and three storeys of flats lie above this. These are organised in four groups running north–south across the site, but the rows are staggered so that this is impossible to perceive. The flats all face west and are set back in section to provide large balconies. Access is via long internal corridors which run the entire length of the site.

The upper parts of the building were clad entirely in Cor-ten weathering steel panels. The run-off from these stained the concrete below and the panels did not perform exactly as predicted. The entire scheme was restored in 1992 when the concrete was painted and many of the panels replaced.

Social democratic pluralism

152Bf Panum Institutet (Copenhagen University Faculty of Medicine) 1971–90

Tagensvej/Blegdamsvej, Nørrebro

KKET (Eva & Nils Koppel, Gert Edstrand, Poul Erik Thyrring)

The planning of this faculty is the institutional equivalent of the 'collective' housing schemes such as Farum Midtpunkt **151**: all the facilities are contained within a single complex organisation. A long building containing offices and other smaller spaces extends along Tagensvej. From this spurs extend to the west at regular intervals and lecture rooms lie between these. Detached from the main organisation, a tall office block is located on Blegdamsvej and the remainder of the triangular site is devoted to car parking.

The most remarkable but inexplicable feature of the long elevation to Tagensvej is the triangular brick wall at the corner with Blegdamsvej from which the more regular pattern emerges.

153Bb Bagsværd Kirke (church) 1974–76

Taxvej, Bagsværd

Jørn Utzon

Skovbrynet

The programme of the new Lutheran churches of the 1960s and 1970s expanded well beyond the mere provision of a hall for preaching, and architects tried various ways of unifying the disparate elements. Utzon's format here encloses all the parts in a long rectangle within two parallel, continuous, rooflit covered ways or ambulatories. The church, meeting rooms and offices lie in a row between the covered ways. Their differing ceiling heights are matched by the height of the ambulatory which steps up and down, reaching its highest at the mid-point of the nave of the church.

In contrast to this orthogonal geometry, the interior of the church proper is spanned by a curved bulging concrete ceiling which is split to accommodate a single large clerestory window. Further but indirect light comes from the roofs of ambulatories which incorporate galleries as they pass the nave. The internal materials include fair-faced reinforced concrete, perforated blockwork and whitened pine fittings. The exterior walls are made entirely of pre-cast concrete panels finished

in semi-glazed and matte white tiles. The roof is of corrugated fibre-cement sheets.

The exterior composition is a great success: while risking looking industrial it avoids the clichés of religiosity or sentimentality. The interior of the church is a conundrum: the two different geometries, the rectangular framework and the bulbous 'clouds' of the ceiling, remain stubbornly separate, and the perforated blockwork screens and much of the mannered detailing now appear merely modish.

4Bi Flexibo housing 1975–76

Følfodvej, Amager

Fællestegnestuen (Viggo Møller-Jensen, Tyge Arnfred, Jørn Ole Sørensen)

[Sundby]

The idea of the 'flexible' dwelling has a history as long as that of modern architecture, and this little scheme is included as a token of architects' continuing experiments with it. The layout is anti-urban: it turns its back on the street and all access is off a new pedestrian street running parallel to Følfodvej. Both sides of this are lined with simple two-storey terraces and a few patio houses. On the exterior the pre-cast concrete panels of which the houses are constructed are successfully disguised with substantial timber outriders: stores, porches and balconies, all well looked after. If the inhabitants have taken advantage of the flexibility offered by the supplied kit of movable partitions, and the interiors are consequently a carnival of dynamic variety, this observer does not know.

5Ac Housing and nursing home 1976

Kronprinsessegade 57A, 59A

Ib and Jørgen Rasmussen

Østerport

The equivalent of two standard blocks of Nyboder **8** housing between Suensonsgade and Gernersgade were combined to accommodate new buildings which extend the plan form and the decorative scheme of the Nyboder terraces, but at a height of three storeys. To the south, new housing is placed in two parallel blocks which depart from the model by having the access at the back on the inside of the block. The dwellings on the upper levels are reached by bridges which span the gap. The same format was employed in the nursing home to the north, but the entrance is provided by a glazed link. The rooms behind face on to an open courtyard and are fully glazed.

☞ The same architects had earlier carried out a conversion of two blocks to the south on Kronprinsessegade between Olfert Fischers Gade and Fredericiagade. These were combined and then rehabilitated with some new buildings, all arranged round and accessed from a new paved square.

Housing

Social democratic pluralism

156Ba **Stavnsholtkirken (church)** 1979–81

Stavnsholtvej 25, Farum

Johan Otto von Spreckelsen

Farum

Von Spreckelsen designed many churches in the Copenhagen area and this is the most noteworthy of them. Two linked complex building blocks occupy a small portion of a characteristically large but characterless suburban site. The smaller is the church proper: square in plan with chamfered corners, and indirectly lit by rooflights set against the external walls. The larger block contains clearly articulated meeting rooms, social spaces and offices laid out round a courtyard.

The work is clearly inspired by that of Louis Kahn, in particular the First Unitarian Church, Rochester, New York, of 1959. Von Spreckelsen, unfortu-

nately, strives for but cannot match the tectonic vigour of his example. The way in which the two blocks meet at their corners to contrive an entrance is particularly unfortunate.

☞ Von Spreckelsen's first church was the **Sankt Nikolaj Kirke** of 1960 at Strøbyvej 2, Hvidovre.

157Bb **Fuglsangpark housing** and **Stenvadskolen (primary school)** 1981–83

Borgmester Jespersens Vej, Farum

Tegnestuen Vandkunsten

Farum

Among the many experimental housing layouts with which Copenhagen has been visited in the twentieth century, those designed by Tegnestuen Vandkunsten are among the more sensible and attractive. This large quarter or small new town is planned on the 'Radburn' principle of a perimeter road serving cul-de-sacs. A small public green space lies between the houses served by each cul-de-sac, and the ends of these greens open out on to a very large sumptuously landscaped park in the centre of the site. The Stenvad primary school, designed by the same architects, lies to the south of the park. The houses, of two and three storeys, were sponsored by a variety of agencies and are of many different types. All, however, are constructed of pre-cast concrete panels artfully disguised with blue paint and the variety of 'hippie' materials, including timber and fibre-cement sheets, and the pointed forms which these architects have made their trademark.

The school, free of prefabrication, is laid out in a similar pattern to that of the housing. A two-storey block containing central services is to the south. North of this across a playground are four groups of classrooms arranged in 'L' or 'U' shapes. The construction and finishes of the school appear even more cheerfully makeshift than those of the housing. Who else but these

Stenvadskolen (primary school)

architects would so casually slice corrugated fibre-cement roofing at so shallow an angle as to produce so sinuous a curve on a gable?

3Be **Novo Industri A/S (pharmaceutical factory)** (1969), 1981–83, 1991
Kroghøvej/Novo Allé, Bagsværd
Dissing + Weitling, successors to Arne Jacobsen

Bagsværd

Novo are Denmark's largest pharmaceutical manufacturer and were among Arne Jacobsen's most consistent patrons. This site contains work from several periods. The large bland factory at the end of Kroghøvej was built in 1969. On either side of the street are buildings completed by Dissing + Weitling after Jacobsen's death, the newest of which are the offices on the right-hand side whose corrugated surface is presented to the street to form a series of courts.

9Ap **Foreign Ministry offices** 1982
Knippelsbro/Strandgade
Halldor Gunnløgsson & Jørgen Nielsen

[Islandsbrygge]

The building of the very unlovely slabs of offices for the Foreign Ministry at the Knippelsbro bridge-head also promoted the restoration of two fine buildings in Christianshavn. The first was **Eigtveds Pakhus**, the warehouse on the north-east side of the dock, and in Strandgade the former head-quarters of the **Asiatic trading company**, designed by Philip de Lange.

Eigtveds Pakhus

Asiatic trading company

60Bf **Unipac (UNICEF distribution centre)** 1983
Unicefplads, Frihavnen
Tegnestuen Vandkunsten

Nordhavn

A large warehouse was converted to provide offices and warehousing for UNICEF's humanitarian relief. All the new materials are from Vandkunsten's 'poor' palette, and mostly black: corrugated fibre-cement, felt and some steel siding.

Social democratic pluralism

161Ak Extension to Det Kongelige Teater (Royal Theatre) 1983–85
Holmens Kanal, Tordenskjoldsgade
Nils Koppel, Knud Holscher, Sven Axelson

 [Kongens Nytorv]

The Royal Theatre **62** was completely renovated from 1983 to 1985 when the foyers and auditorium were redecorated and everything to the south of the proscenium was completely rebuilt. Most of the existing façades to Holmens Kanal were preserved, but this new one at the former number 5 was expensively rebuilt and finished in sandstone overlaid with bronze sun screens.

162B(b) Courtyard houses 1983–86
Hulsø Ege 1–7, Rungsted Kyst
Tage Lyneborg

 Rungsted Kyst

The courtyard houses at Kingo near Helsingør, designed by Jørn Utzon in 1958, exercised a powerful influence in both Denmark and beyond. They spawned many reworkings, of which this, although small, is one of the best by an architect who has specialised in housing design. Four single-storey houses in white brick, two with straight plans, two with L-shaped, are set on a slope facing south over a small pond. Their courtyards are separated from the open space round the pond by low stepped walls. The whole provides a compelling vision of suburban community.

☞ To the south, at Pinjehøj 1–8 on the other side of Rungstedvej is a group of single storey **houses** of 1961–62 designed by Jørgen Bo & Vlhelm Wohlert, the architects of the Louisiana Art Gallery and Museum **138**, and using the same white brick walls and timber roofs. The **Klubhus, Kongelig Dansk Yachtklub and Rungsted Kyst Sejlklub** (yacht and sailing clubs) is on the coast at Rungsted Havn 46, Rungsted Kyst. The long black-clad shed was designed in 1979–80 by Harald Grut & Søren Borg Nielsen.

163Ba Crimpgården offices 1984–85
Solvang 30, Allerød
Tegnestuen Vandkunsten

Cheerful brutalism is brought to an otherwise standard business park by these offices. The one-and-a-half-storey shed accommodates one full floor of offices and a small mezzanine, the section wrapped into a square looking out over a central garden. The materials are those characteristic of these architects: deeply corrugated white fibre-cement cladding on the outside roof (or is it a battered wall?) and blue-painted steel panels on the pointed shapes that mark the entrance.

64Be **Sibeliusparken housing** 1984–86

Tæbyvej/Egegårdsvej, Rødovre

Fællestegnestuen (Jørn Ole Sørensen, Tyge Arnfred & Viggo Møller-Jensen)

Jyllingevej

The scheme was built in two phases. The first, to the north, was an irregular street lined with two-and three-storey houses and wrapped round three sides of the site. The land left over at the edges is used for allotments and the central space is a landscaped park. In the design of the layout and the houses, particular attention was given to energy-saving measures, including glazed winter gardens to the living rooms.

The materials are mundane: red brick for the ground-floor walls, battened fibre-cement for the

first and second storeys and corrugated fibre-cement roofing.

☞ To the east, a poignant contrast: the dense, ugly blocks of flats from the late 1990s show what is subsequently being provided for the housing market, or what buyers have been persuaded to want.

65Bd **Experimental housing quarter, Egebjerggård** 1985–96

Skovvej, Ballerup

Colom & Gudmand-Høyer, master plan; Susse Fischer, Henning Larsen, Boje Lundgaard & Lene Tranberg, Tage Lyneborg, Tegnestuen Vandkunsten and other architects

Ballerup

Development of the large roughly rectangular site as a housing exhibition has proceeded in four stages, starting at the north, and is served by a single main road. Four groups of housing are strung along this, the latest, to the south-east, completed to coincide with the 'Copenhagen, European City of Culture 1996' event. The intention was to provide a district of mixed uses and for different sorts of people, and this has been realised as an assemblage of 'something for everybody': wildly different types of housing in an astonishing variety of architectural styles and forms, although none are higher than four storeys. The first three groups are informally arranged round cul-de-sacs. The last, still under construction in 1997, has a more strict layout arranged round an axis which is closed to the south by a pair of electricity pylons. Works of integrated art are scattered (carefully placed) throughout the site, notably the three parallel arched brick walls by Per Kirkeby, but what it really needs is the maturing of the landscape to soften the architectural oppositions of what is in fact a suburb. The most recent and stylish schemes include Tegnestuen Vandkunsten's short three-storey terrace covered in their favourite black fibre-cement sheets; Tage Lyneborg's neo-brutalist

Terrace by Tegnestuen Vandkunsten

Row by Tage Lyneborg

Social democratic pluralism

row in brick and with corrugated fibre-cement roofing; and lovers of organic architecture will seek out the lonely, earthbound Vingehuset ('Wing house') by the lake, designed in 1990 by Niels Guttormsen with Colom and Gudmand-Høyer.

Vingehuset ('Wing house')

166Bf Paustian A/S (furniture showroom and warehouse) 1986–87

Kalkbrænderiløbskaj 2

Utzon Associates

Nordhavn

The furniture showroom and warehouse together occupy a single building under an asymmetrically pitched roof. The showroom is on three floors arranged round a well lit from a large rooflight in the ridge of the roof. The columns have angled brackets at their junctions with the lateral beams which support the roof and eaves. These brackets are the residue of Utzon's poetic metaphor for the structure: that of a forest. The structure consists entirely of beautifully fabricated and placed pre-cast concrete components, all painted a blinding white. (A *white* 'forest'?)

167Bf Housing, Garvergården 1986–88

Jagtvej 211/Masnedøgade, Østerbro

Tegnestuen Vandkunsten

Svanemøllen

Many of the buildings Vandkunsten designed were for suburban or greenfield sites: this is one of their few schemes built in an urban context. The design unfortunately confirms that the tendency of their work is towards the anti-urban. A corner of a block in the nineteenth-century city is blown open by a serpentine slab of housing lying along Masnedøgade, and is left looking like a stranded portion of a village. The space between this slab and the existing warehouse to the east is made public and used for access to the various dwellings. The finishings and their arrangement are as adventurous here as elsewhere in these architects' work: irregularly coursed white fibre-cement sheets separated by pink-painted metal strips, and a glowering black-felt roof.

68Bi København Lufthavn I Kastrup (Airport buildings) 1986–91, 1994–95

Kastrup

KHR A/S Arkitekter; Arkitektfirmaet Chr. P. Skjoldborg; Holm & Grut Arkitekter and others

Kastrup

In 1997, the airport at Kastrup was undergoing one of the convulsions of reconstruction which seem permanently to afflict all such structures, the newest one including a motorway extension and works to a new metro station and railway terminus which will eventually be connected to the new Øresund crossing. All the extensions so far have been additive: very little has been demolished and the first terminal of 1939, designed by Vilhelm Lauritzen, is still in use. A new one was added in 1960. In the early 1980s, a master plan by Skaarup & Jespersen provided a framework for extension. The most recent buildings within this include the domestic terminal of 1988 and its associated parking garage of 1990 (illustrated), both by KHR. The latter has round towers enclosing ramps at the corners and is clad particularly felicitously in fritted glass panels. The various concourses and links have been designed by different firms including Concourse A by Holm & Grut and Concourse C by Christian P. Skjoldborg.

69Be Viften ('The Fan' cultural centre) 1988

Rødovre Parkvej, Rødovre

Dissing + Weitling

Rødovre

Jacobsen's Town hall and Public Library formed two sides of a square. This later building forms a third and closes the square to the north. Its forms and materials contrast strongly with those of Jacobsen's transatlantic cool treatment: the auditorium projects upwards and is covered in crinkly lead. The foyers extend from it in a fan shape.

☞ The Rådhus (Town Hall) **136** of 1955 and the Public Library **150** of 1969 were both designed by Arne Jacobsen.

70Am Tycho Brahe Planetarium 1988–89

Gammel Kongevej 10

Knud Munk ApS

Vesterport

For once Munk's favourite cylindrical form nearly suits its function, the planetarium's domed auditorium. The stripy brickwork is possibly just postmodern decoration, but its angles do rhyme with those of the pointed site.

Social democratic pluralism

171 Bi **Skelgårdskirken (church)** 1988–89
Sinding(s)vej 3–13, Kastrup
Tegnestuen Møllen ApS (Gert Ingemann, Jørn Pedersen, Claes Høgly & Jens Rosenkjær)

This church conveniently faces the large car parking area of the shops nearby. Its arrangement is artful or confused: the single-storey lean-to accommodation of the entrance side is split to provide an entrance and runs parallel to the main axis of the nave with its dominant monopitch roof. The entrance is marked by the tower which spans the full width of the nave. The axes are unresolved and the results far from satisfactory.

172B(a) **Housing, Allerødhave** 1988–90
Allerødvej 27, Allerød
Boje Lundgaard & Lene Tranberg

Allerød

This small enclave is included to show how far fashions in housing layouts changed between, say, 1970 and 1990. Although 'collective' to the extent that it is an enclave, a single design and that most of the parts are joined to one another, the emphasis is on the bourgeois norm. The outer three-storey terrace forms a ring of dwellings placed directly on the ground. Inside the ring are further two-storey dwellings. The style, complete with ventilators sentimentally disguised as 'chimneys', was characterised by Danish critics as 'English', but to an English eye it appears more North American.

173B(c) **Vedbæk Havn (marina)** 1988–90
Strandvejen, Vedbæk
Tegnestuen Vandkunsten

Vedbæk

Marinas are not often laid out by architects, but Vandkunsten won a competition for the design of this one. The site is neatly organised: a car park runs along its length parallel to the shore and next to this is the promenade which provides access to the regularly spaced piers. Buildings housing the various functions of the marina are placed at the beginning of each pier. Those at the ends are of three storeys, those in between of one. The materials are both appropriately nautical but probably what these architects would have used anyway: black fibre-cement siding and horizontal timber boarding, black felt roofs.

4B(b) **Egedal Kirke (church)** 1990
Egedalsvej 3, Kokkedal
Fogh & Følner Arkitektfirma

Kokkedal

Fogh & Følner are among those architects who have found a suitable format for accommodating the extensive programmatic requirements of the modern Danish Lutheran church. The architectural problem, also faced by e.g. Utzon at **153** and von Spreckelsen at **156**, is to give suitable prominence to the nave of the church while uniting this with the many other spaces, entrance, meeting and confirmation instruction rooms and offices for staff and clergy. On a fine site, the accommodation here is arranged round three sides of a small court whose fourth open side faces the landscaped churchyard. The monopitch lead-finished roofed volumes range in height from the bell tower, the highest, to the next highest, the church proper, to the lowest, the meeting rooms.

The predominant material of the exterior is a cream brick with inset bands of white glazed brick, and aluminium window frames. Internally, the brick is painted, and the frames and fittings are of blond beech. The interior of the church is a great success, spare, calm and well lit, and of no identifiable style. (The altar fittings are by Bent Exner, brother of one of the architects Exner.) Generally, the only residue of what may be the period's postmodernism is in the stripy exterior and the mannered diagonals of the window frames.

☞ About a kilometre to the south at Ved Stampedammen, Usserød, is a further example of a **courtyard housing** layout influenced by that at Kingo of 1958–60 by Jørn Utzon, but built of

white brick and with flat roofs. The atrium houses of 1965 were designed by Carl R. Frederiksen, Mogens Hammer, Henning Moldenhawer and Hubert Paulsen.

Social democratic pluralism

175Ad **Extension to Østerport Station, and shops**
1990–91

Oslo Plads/Østbanegade

KHR AS Arkitekter (Knud Holscher, Svend Axelsson & Jan Søndergaard) with Danish Railways Construction Service

Østerport

The original station is to the north. The extension provided accommodation for new access to the platforms and for shops at street level. The engineering work to the new circulation is neatly done, but the shops lie behind a redundant fair-faced concrete screen which breaks free to display itself inadequately to the corner with Østbanegade.

☞ **'Den Frie Udstillings Bygning'**, the little wooden pavilion on the opposite, south side of the road occasionally houses architectural and art exhibitions.

176Ak **BT Huset (newspaper offices)** 1993–94

Kristen Bernikow Gade 6/Grønnegade

Henning Larsens Tegnestue

Nørreport

The newest building for the tabloid edition of 'the world's oldest newspaper', *Berlingske Tidende*, provides a small amount of office accommodation on five floors and a penthouse and a cheerful stylish addition to Copenhagen's streetscape. The façades are entirely glazed but those to Kristen Bernikow Gade are screened by perforated metal panels inset with a grid of tiny red 'BT' logos which light up at night.

☞ Two of *Berlingske Tidende*'s earlier buildings **99** are diagonally opposite.

7B(a) **Engholmkirken (church)** 1993–94
Engholm Kirkevej 1, Allerød
CUBO

Allerød

Different architects working with the Lutheran church programme have tried different strategies for uniting the various elements. Here the church, offices and meeting rooms are housed in individual volumes and all except the bell tower connected by a pergola. This is laid diagonally across the ample site and terminates in a sunken garden to the east. The rectangular forms are clean-cut and modern, and finished in fine cream stone and white rendering. The interior of the church is plain and surprisingly intimate. The most noteworthy feature of the design, however, will eventually be the landscaping: the site has been lavishly planted with small forests of oaks.

78Bb **Offices for E. Pihl & Søn** 1993–94
Nybrovej 116, Vangede
KHR (Knud Holscher and others)

Lyngby

The offices for a construction company are on an unremarkable site and set back from the nondescript street. Two L-shaped single ranges of offices lie on either side of a corridor. At their ends, one range slides past the other in the manner of Kay Fisker's plans, see **135** for example. Connecting the corridors, a three-storey high atrium lies at the crook of the 'L'. The staff canteen is treated separately and housed in its own trapezoidal building which projects into the garden to which much of the site is devoted. The style is crisply modern, although slightly mannered in the patterns of brickwork and flush windows, and the materials well handled, especially in the canteen's beautiful lead cladding panels.

9B(b) **Forskningscenter for Skov og Landskab (Danish Forest & Landscape Institute)** 1995
Hørsholm Kongevej 11, Hørsholm
Gehrdt Bornebusch Tegnestue

Rungsted Kyst

The building contains only the offices of the institute: no trees are handled on the premises. Two two-storey cranked rows of single-banked offices are placed back to back. The space in between houses circulation, and at one end on the ground floor is the entrance, at the other the canteen. The architectural treatment is elaborate and lavish: diaphragm brick walls with a brushed mortar finish separate the glazed corridors from the offices on the other side. In a surprising return of the hippie 'telegraph-pole' style, these are entirely constructed of and clad in timber and lean against the walls. The views from the building are delightfully and appropriately sylvan, and the only disappointment is the siting: the building is first viewed and approached from an undistinguished suburban traffic roundabout.

Social democratic pluralism

180Ao Extension to Royal Library from 1995
Christiansbrygge
Schmidt, Hammer & Lassen

The first royal library was founded by Frederik III.
The present red-brick building was built at the end
of one of Christian IV's docks in 1898–1906 and
designed by Hans J. Holm. It presented its back
to the water from which it was separated by the
traffic on Christiansbrygge. The design for the
new extension was won in a competition set in the
context of a master plan for the waterfront extending south from the library. The new building
(incomplete in 1997) consists of two parts. The
first part is a new shallow strip of accommodation
on the back of the existing library; a large new
block between road and water is connected to
this by a bridge. This block includes a new library,
a hall for concerts and lectures, exhibition galleries, a café and the inevitable shop. The design
was self-consciously up-to-date: all the external
walls of the new free-standing building lean, some
of them outwards, but the enormously cumber-
some structures which enable this are hidden by
the polished black-granite facings.

181Al Arkitekternes Hus 1995–96
Strandgade 27, Christianshavn
Nielsen, Nielsen & Nielsen

[Islandsbrygge]

There are two buildings here. The block facing
the street contains additional offices for the
Foreign Ministry whose main building **159** is at the
southern end of Strandgade. Behind this, and
separated from it by a full-height atrium containing the stairs, are the offices of the Danish Union
of Architects and the Arkitektens Forlag (architectural publishers). Each building has a different
architectural treatment. The offices to the street
are finished in white rendering overlaid with a
partly redundant metal sunscreen, while behind
this the architects' offices are housed in a timber-
clad shell inside a glass box. The space at the
back of the site, which also gives access to
Gammel Dok **65**, has been landscaped.

2Bf Offices, shops and housing, ex **Tuborg Brewery** from 1995

Tuborgvej/Strandvejen, Hellerup

Henning Larsens Tegnestue and other architects

Hellerup

The Tuborg Brewery closed in the early 1990s and the large site which extends between Strandvejen and the Sound is being developed in stages. The former headquarters building **87** was converted into lettable offices, and the land to the north laid out as a mixed use scheme with offices, shops and housing. The master plan for this site was eminently sensible and conventional: buildings of modest height face Strandvejen, and Tuborgvej was reordered as a tree-lined boulevard which will give access to subsequent phases of the redevelopment. The new buildings, mostly clad in mortarbrushed brickwork, are pleasantly dull, and the most notable architectural feature, designed by Henning Larsens Tegnestue, is the conical white **Rotunden** which, placed at the slight bend in Strandvejen, the main road, supplies a beacon for the whole redevelopment. The rotunda is, however, empty, providing access only to the supermarket beyond and, via a lift or spiral ramp, to the small restaurant at its summit.

3Aj Information centre 1996

Rådhuspladsen

KHR

Hovedbanegården

Built as an information centre for the event 'Copenhagen, European City of Culture 1996', this extensive kiosk now provides data about the city's excellent bus services. Urbanistically it serves to separate the square in front of the Rådhus, reordered in the same year, from the bus stops to its north. Its provocative architectural restlessness served its original function well, its present one less so: a 2-metre high wall would now do.

Social democratic pluralism

184Bh Museet for Moderne Kunst 'Arket'
(Museum of Modern Art 'The Ark') 1994–96
Skovej 42, Ishøj
Søren Robert Lund

Ishøj, and bus to Ishøj Strand

The 'museum' was intended as Denmark's first multi-media centre, and as well as conventional galleries it includes a concert hall and cinema. Its design was won in competition by its then young architect who intended the building to be placed in the dunes and nearer the shore line than its present position. The various spaces are arranged on either side of a very long wall. On its seaward side are the entrance, foyer, concert hall, a long rooflit gallery and at first floor a restaurant with sea views. On the land side rectangular-shaped rooflit galleries extend from the wall. The separate circulations of these two are connected by a red-painted concrete tunnel. On the flat site, the various arbitrary changes of level between one gallery and another, each of which has to be provided with arrangements for those with disabilities to negotiate, make the planning enormously clumsy and using the building more irritating than it might have been.

This was one of Europe's first built examples of the 'deconstructed' architectural manner, and its realisation suggests that this were better left on paper or in architects' or philosophers' minds. There are two difficulties: first, that the pointed and crescent shapes which may seem appealing on drawings look less appetising when realised in the ordinary materials of which buildings are necessarily built and, second, that these shapes are very difficult to build, and in some cases impossible even with Danish craftsmanship, as various patently unfinished and unfinishable parts of the building pathetically demonstrate.

☞ The coast on which the museum stands is a part result of the **Køge Bugt** land reclamation and recreational master plan, commissioned in 1977. This proposed a 5-kilometre (8-mile) long coastal park to complement Copenhagen's existing narrow pebbly beaches along the Sound to the north. The large polygonally profiled power station visible along the coast to the east and standing on its made-up land is the **Avedøre Kraftvarmeværk** of 1985–91. The architects were Claus Bjarrum with Jørgen Hauxner.

185Bi Øresund crossing started 1997
Denmark–Sweden

With a project very similar to the crossing of the Storebælt between the Danish islands of Fyn and Sjælland it is proposed to construct a nearly 16-kilometre (9.7-mile) long road and rail crossing of the Sound between Amager near Kastrup Airport and the coast of Sweden. One section will be built on a causeway, another on an island. The railway line will then tunnel under the Sound while a road will cross it carried on a bridge with a span of nearly half a kilometre (a third of a mile).

Excursions

The following can easily be visited on a day trip from Copenhagen, and provide either contrast or supplement to its architectural history. Frequent trains to each of them leave from Hovedbanegården, Copenhagen's central railway station.

Louisiana Humlebæk, 30 km (20 miles) north of Copenhagen
This beautiful art museum lies well outside Copenhagen but is included in the text at **138**. A ticket combining train travel and entrance fee can be obtained from the Hovedbanegården. If travelling by car the visitor can combine a visit to Louisiana with one to Fredensborg Palæ **22**, 10 km (about 6 miles) to the west.

Dragør Amager, 12 km (about 7 miles) southeast of Copenhagen
The former fishing village, now the port for ferries between Copenhagen and Malmö in Sweden, was regularised in the second half of the eighteenth century. Much of the fabric of rows of modest single-storey cottages survives, gentrified in the twentieth century. The arrangement of single-sided streets may have been the model for later housing schemes in Copenhagen such as Henningsen and Bentsen's Bakkehusene housing **94**.

Roskilde 30 km (20 miles) west of Copenhagen
Of older foundation than Copenhagen, Roskilde lies by an inlet on the island of Sjælland. The small and unremarkable town which straggles along its main street is dominated by its **Cathedral** built of brick and commissioned in 1170 by Bishop Absalon at about the same time as he was having Copenhagen's first castle **1** built. Absalon's scheme was not realised and the nave was continued in French style and completed at the end of the fourteenth century. Several chapels were subsequently extended from the aisles. The most spectacular of these is the royal chapel

designed by H. C. Harsdorff and built 1774–1825 to house the tomb of Frederik V, but which has since been used as the burial place for most of Denmark's monarchs. Its plan is a Greek-cross surmounted by a dome and approached from the aisle through a screen in Harsdorff's favourite Ionic order. Frederik IX who died in 1972 chose not to be buried alongside his successors, and his tomb is housed in the small brick enclosure to the left of the cathedral's main door. This was designed by the Exners, Inger and Johannes, architects of many churches including Præstebro **147**.

Next to the cathedral, to the east, lies the royal and very yellow **Gule Palæ (Yellow Palace)**, designed by Laurids de Thurah and built in 1733. The main two-storey block is flanked by wings and approached through a gated stable block. To the north is the area of Roskilde's former port, now being transformed into a resort and marina. Next to this is the **Vikingeskibshallen (Viking Ship Museum)** completed in 1968 and designed by Erik Christian Sørensen to house the extensive remains of three Viking ships excavated from the mud at the bottom of the inlet which the museum overlooks. The building is an academic brutalist construction in exposed reinforced concrete. In the summer its exterior can be viewed from the sea by taking a small voyage in a replica Viking ship.

Vikingeskibshallen (Viking Ship Museum), interior

117

Vocabulary

Danish	English
bro	bridge
dronning	queen
gade	street
gammel	old
gård	yard, court
havn	harbour
hjørnet	corner
hus	house
kirke	church
konge	king
kro	inn
lille	small
nord	north
ny	new
plads	square
port	gate, door
sankt	saint
skole	school
slot	castle, palace
stor	big
syd	south
sø	lake
torv	square
vej	way, street
vest	east
ø	island
øst	west

Select bibliography

Kim Dirckinck-Holmfield, *Guide 2 to Danish Architecture 1960–1995* (Arkitektens Forlag, Copenhagen, 1995)

Tobias Faber, *Architektur in Dänemark* (Det Danske Selskab, Copenhagen, 1978)

Peter Høeg, *Miss Smilla's Feeling for Snow* (Harvill, London, 1993)—for a resident's description of Copenhagen in winter.

Helge Seidelin Jacobsen, *An Outline History of Denmark* (Høst & Søn, Copenhagen, 1986)

W. Glyn Jones and Kirsten Gade, *Blue Guide Denmark* (A & C Black, London, 1992)

Jørgen Sestoft and Jørgen Hegner Christiansen, *Guide to Danish Architecture 1000–1960* (Arkitektens Forlag, Copenhagen, 1991)

Author's acknowledgements

I should like to thank the following people who offered valuable advice, navigation, help and criticism: Michael Ellison, James Cummins, Christoph Grafe and Simon Ingvartsen.

Illustration credits

The photographs and drawings are by the author with the exception of **93**, lower, which is by Christoph Grafe.

Index

Index

Index

Map A Central Copenhagen

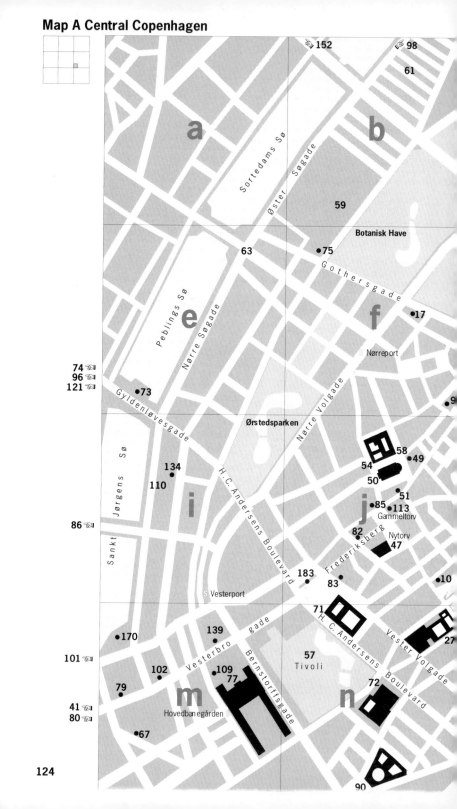

Sortedams Sø

Øster Søgade

152

98

61

59

Botanisk Have

a

b

63

•75

Gothersgade

Peblings Sø

Nørre Søgade

e

f

•17

Nørreport

74
96
121

Gyldenløvesgade

•73

Nørre Volgade

•9

Ørstedsparken

Sankt Jørgens Sø

•134

110

i

58
•49

54

50

86

H.C. Andersens Boulevard

51
•85
•113
Gammeltorv

j

82

Nytorv
47

Frederiksberg

183

83

•10

S Vesterport

71

27

Vester Volgade

•170

139

101

Vesterbrogade

Bernstorffsgade

57
Tivoli

H.C. Andersens Boulevard

72

102

•109
77

79

m

n

41
80

Hovedbanegården

•67

90

124

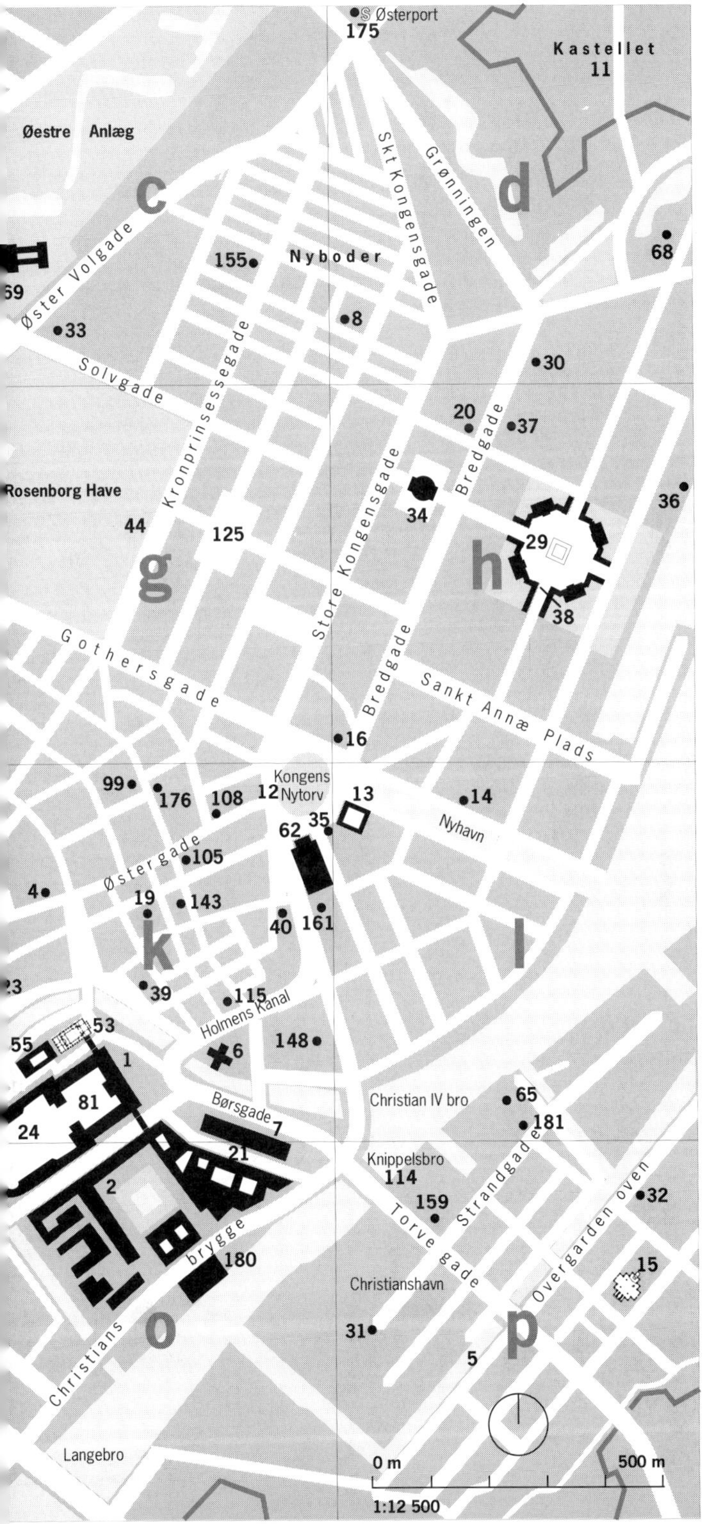

S Østerport
175

Kastellet
11

Øestre Anlæg

c

d

Skt Kongensgade

Grønningen

155

Nyboder

68

Øster Volgade

59

33

8

30

Solvgade

Kronprinsessegade

20

Bredgade

37

Rosenborg Have

44

125

34

36

g

Store Kongensgade

29

h

38

Gothersgade

Bredgade

Sankt Annæ Plads

16

99

176

108

12 Kongens
Nytorv

13

14

62

35

Nyhavn

Østergade

105

4

19

143

40

161

k

l

23

39

115

Holmens Kanal

55

53

6

148

1

Børsgade

Christian IV bro

65

81

7

181

24

21

Knippelsbro

114

32

2

159

Strandgade

Torvegade

Overgarden oven

180

brygge

15

Christians

o

Christianshavn

p

31

5

Langebro

0 m   500 m

1:12 500

Map B Outer Copenhagen

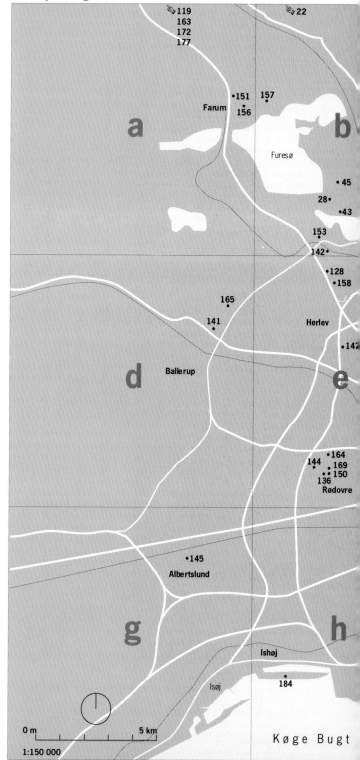

119
163
172
177

22

•151   157
•
156

a   b

Farum

Furesø

•45

28•
•43

153
•
142•

•128
•158

165
•

141   Herlev
•

•147

d   Ballerup   e

•164
144   •169
•   •150
136
Rødovre

•145
Albertslund

g   h

Ishøj

Isøj   •
184

0 m   5 km
Køge Bugt

1:150 000

52
174
179

162

138
173

erød

C

25
Dyrehave

22

107
112• 140
131

gby
8

Klampenborg

116•

97 104
48
Hellerup

Gladsaxe
137•

•93 182
76 •87
46 • 78•• 91
127• 89•70
Bispebjerg
95 Østerbro
123• •84 149
111• •120 •135
167•
56
130 100 • 160 •166
noj • Nørrebro 152 •98
94•
•88
92• 60
96 • 74
42 121•
86• Map A
Frederiksberg 101•
•18 80
41 • • •26
66• 64
•103 Amagerbro
133•

Øresund

f

117
• •
118

Kastrup
•154 171•

i

185

168
Lufthavn

Dragør